NEXT GENERATION TRIBUTE BOOK

JAMES VAN HISE

Library of Congress Cataloging-in-Publication Data
James Van Hise, 1949

TREK: THE NEXT GENERATION TRIBUTE BOOK

1. TREK: THE NEXT GENERATION TRIBUTE BOOK (television, popular culture)
I. Title

Published by Pioneer Books, Inc., 5715 N. Balsam Rd., Las Vegas, NV, 89130.

First Printing, 1993

DEDICATED TO
GENE
RODDENBERRY

EDITED AND DESIGNED BY
Hal Schuster
WITH THE ASSISTANCE OF
David Lessnick
COVER PAINTING BY
Morris Scott Dollens

CONTENTS

THE NEXT GENERATION: 6 YEARS AND COUNTING

The fall of 1993 begins the seventh season of STAR TREK: THE NEXT GENERATION, an unprecedented measure of success for this spin-off from the original '60s television series. By all accounts this will probably be the final season of the series. Sources indicate that after seven years and more than 180 episodes, the cast and crew of THE NEXT GENERATION will take the next step to the motion picture screen. It would be nice if they could at least make it an annual event instead of the two to three years which have fallen between the STAR TREK motion pictures produced to date. After proving they can do 26 hours a year, 2 hours a year should be a snap.

When THE NEXT GENERATION premiered in 1987 it was greeted with about as much skepticism as it was applause. It had a lot to live up to. But before his death in 1991, Gene Roddenberry saw his creation of THE NEXT GENERATION eclipse Trek Classic in popularity, as well as numerically.

STAR TREK has proven to be far more viable than even its most enthusiastic fans granted it back in the dog days of the '70s when calls to revive the series seemed to be falling on deaf ears. Now in 1993, 20 years after the first STAR TREK convention ever held (in New York City), there is more STAR TREK than anyone could have hoped for. Six movies, 79 episodes of Classic Trek, more than 150 episodes of THE NEXT GENERATION, 18 episodes of DEEP SPACE NINE, and you can bet that if DEEP SPACE NINE manages to last more than two seasons that another spin-off will be spun out of STAR TREK gold.

Many of you are recent converts to the STAR TREK universe, while others, such as myself, were there in front of the TV set in 1966 and pushing for its return a decade later.

Who would have thought that we'd not only win, but win so big?

———JAMES VAN HISE
June 3, 1993

Patrick Stewart enjoying himself at the Video Software Dealers Association convention in Las Vegas in July 1992

Photo credit: ©1993 Ron Galella Ltd.

CHAPTER 1

MEET THE STARS

Gene Roddenberry on Dec. 20, 1990 attending a screening of
"Godfather III" at the Academy of Motion Picture Arts and Sciences.

Let's turn back the time to 1987 when a highly anticipated new television series was finally beginning. What's particularly interesting about this piece is that it was actually written in 1987 looking forward rather than in 1993 looking back. This is one person's impression of "Encounter At Farpoint" the night it first aired.

CHAPTER 1
THE NEXT GENERATION: PREMIERE NIGHT

By Jefferson Swycaffer

I got a rare treat the other day. I got to watch the premiere of STAR TREK. It was quite a lot of fun. I liked the fire-eating young captain, and the cool, dignified first officer. I liked the whole crew. I also liked the plot; it was a nice blend of science fiction and 'fantasy.' And my spine tingled with delight at the opening narration by William Shatner: "Space. The Final Frontier."

Yes, I liked "Where No Man Has Gone Before."

It's very rare for me to find a STAR TREK episode I hadn't already seen. I honestly thought I'd seen them all. But I hadn't. I was flipping across the channels, and there they were: Kirk and Spock. And suddenly I sat bolt upright and realized the scene and the plot were new!

The very next evening, I was able to repeat this rare and delicious treat. I got to watch STAR TREK: THE NEXT GENERATION in its premiere episode. And you know something? I liked it too.

This unique perspective gave me a bit of insight into what we can expect. It also afforded me a slight advantage in judging the new show. Old Trek ("Classic Trek") grew by leaps and bounds as the cast began to flesh out their characters. McCoy was brought in, and he added to the chemistry. The sets and the uniforms were spruced up. The plots explored new ideas and ideals.

New Trek, then, can also be expected to grow. We haven't seen the full scope of what we're really being offered. We've got a treat in store for us.

THE NEXT GENERATION— A FIRST LOOK

The crew is magnificent. Captain Picard is a seasoned leader, portrayed by a seasoned actor. The role is strong. The actor, Patrick Stewart, has been a Shakespearean actor for many years. Can't you just see him as Julius Caesar? Captain Kirk was an iron fist in a velvet glove (some would say he was an iron fist inside a rubber muppet). Picard reverses the notion, and gives us a tougher exterior, but a gentler interior. I could conceive people questioning Kirk's orders. Not Picard's.

The First Officer, Number One, Mister Mate, this Riker fellow. . . did you notice how much he looked like William Shatner? He's the guy who gets to leap over boulders, body-slam alien scum, kiss the woman, shoot his partner from cover, and generally tear around like an Apache. He's fun. This guy's a regular Li'l Abner.

What they've done, you see, is take Jim Kirk and split him in two. (No, not the way it happened in "The Enemy Within"). The captain

is now the Old Man, old iron-britches, the guy who narrows his eyes and clenches his fist and sends young men off to their deaths. The Exec is now the Young Man, who exercises all the prerogatives of youth. I expect this to become the central dramatic tension of the show. This should easily outweigh the tension we saw between Kirk and Spock; this has some real meat on its bones. The Oedipal implications alone are truly staggering. Did you notice that both men are romancing the medical officer, each in his own rough way?

The Chief Medical Officer is also a very powerful dramatic tool here. (I also expect that "CMO" will enter the Trekkie lexicon and phrase book, alongside "Phaser" and "Two to beam up"). She's an outsider, a Jill-come-lately. She respects the hell out of the Captain, and she admires the Exec. Gee, aren't romantic triangles fun?

FINAL CONSENSUS

The rest of the crewmembers are also fun. They could make a damn fine superhero team in a Marvel comic book. There's the information-gatherer: Geordie LaForge, the blind guy with the specs. There's the "brain": Data, the android with perfect recall. There's the "brick" — two of them, in fact: Tasha Yar, the security officer and Worf, the Klingon, who split the role but who compliment each other deliciously. There's Wesley, the dumb-as-dirt kid, and Troi, the sex-objectified woman. There's another guy, the spear-carrier whom everyone overlooks (I don't even recall his name: a faceless extra who just happens to have a face). And, of course, there's the ship itself, always a major star in any STAR TREK show. (I would like to see an episode that emphasizes Tasha Yar, the security officer, who's a bitch, and Worf, the Klingon, who's a bastard. Those two hot-heads butting against one another—ah, what a show that would be. I frankly have to say that feisty, trim, quick-mouthed Yar is my favorite character in the show).

The plot? Okay, the plot had holes. It was two plots, actually, poorly stapled together. The business with "Q" calling a kangaroo court and making a lot of snide comments about humanity: ho hum. We've seen it all before. But the other plot, the business about the goings-on at Far Point. . . that was a good, solid, thought-provoking STAR TREK plot. There was deceit, a mystery, a sensible solution which was, in fact, legitimately portrayed and presaged, and a heart-warming climax (provided in brilliant backlighting by Industrial Light & Magic). Sure, the plotting was the weakest part of the show. They need to spend a bit more money and time on the writing.

Good stuff. You can pick holes in it but half of Old Trek was pretty stupid, and some was utter garbage—an "Omega Glory" for every "City on the Edge of Forever," and a "Spock's Brain" for each "Errand of Mercy." We watched the show grow into its full promise—and sometimes we watched it fall grievously short.

I'm gonna be spending time in front of the old boob tube.

CHAPTER 2

Brent Spiner and Wil Wheaton at the L.A. TNG Tribute on March 14, 1992.

Brent Spiner all dressed up at the wedding of Marina Sirtis held
June 21, 1992 at the St. Sophia Cathedral in Los Angeles.

Although STAR TREK: THE NEXT GENERATION premiered in 1987, Brent Spiner waited two years before he felt comfortable with the idea of appearing in public. He'd guarded his privacy to such a degree before this that he'd even requested that publications not print photos of him, out of makeup, from his pre-TNG acting appearances.

CHAPTER 2

BRENT SPINER— IN PERSON

By Diana Collins

Brent Spiner, alias Mr. Data, made his first U.S. convention appearance at the Penta Hotel in Manhattan, New York, at 8:10 p.m. on Friday and Saturday nights during Thanksgiving weekend, November 24th & 25th, 1989. Introducing him was Richard Arnold, Creation Convention guest speaker and STAR TREK slide show presenter for the daytime schedule of events. As Brent Spiner stepped on stage, a very enthusiastic audience gave him a standing ovation which lasted several minutes. He responded by blushing, thanking everyone and making repeated hand gestures to show his appreciation.

Having quieted approximately 800 people in the Grand Ballroom (Saturday night alone), Brent Spiner spoke about his background, acting career before STAR TREK, and his insights on the behind-the-scenes events leading to the filming of the show. He also spent an hour answering questions from the audience.

Because Brent had requested that no cameras or audio/videotaping equipment be present during his performance, this reporter took copious notes with pad and pen. Included are some highlights taken from the question and answer dialogue during the Saturday night performance from my fifth row, center aisle seat only 20 feet away. I've inserted audience responses and comments in parenthesis in an attempt to recreate the ambiance of Mr. Spiner's Saturday evening performance.

ON STAGE

Microphone in hand, Spiner glided across the stage, sporting the same hairstyle and round gold framed glasses he wore during his Oscar night TONIGHT SHOW appearance with Jay Leno. He was dressed in a tailored suit accented by a black turtleneck and black suede shoes. His first words to the audience were, "Once again I'm feeling like Elvis." He began crooning, "Are you lonesome tonight?" his tenor voice achieving a decent fake Elvis vocal quality to audience applause. Next he asked, "Can you imagine thousands of Brent Spiner imitations years from now? And how do you know that I'm not one now?"

Brent Spiner's "lounge act" was on a roll as he quickly changed accents with the routine. Repeating his line, "Good evening ladies and germs!" from his comedic TNG episode with Joe Piscopo, Spiner next faked a British accent used in his cameo appearance in WHAT'S ALAN WATCHING? introducing imaginary Beatles on stage behind him.

Warmed up, Spiner exclaimed, "It's great to be back in New York and on stage again! I miss being on the stage and would like to think that I have at least one play in me…perhaps even a musical. Did anyone see any of my musicals?"

Fans yelled names—"Sunday in the Park With George," "Big River," "The Three Musketeers," and finally WHAT'S ALAN WATCHING? Spiner quipped, "That's not a musical!" amid audience snickers.

"I shopped before the Con for an overcoat in Barnies men's store in Manhattan, for obvious reasons. I had never needed one in L.A."

SPINER: "A clerk approached to wait on me."

CLERK: "You look familiar but I can't seem to place you."

SPINER: "Okay, I'll give you a hint. I'm an actor." The clerk scratched his head. "I'll give you a second hint, I'm on television." The clerk pondered further without success. "Okay, this will definitely give it away. On television you'd probably notice that I have a green hue."

CLERK: He suddenly burst out, "Oh, you're Lou Ferrigno!"

SPINER: Sly expression and eyebrows arched, "Yes I am. How'd you guess!" To which the audience howled.

BRENT'S CO-STARS

Questions from the audience were many and varied but started by asking about the cast of THE NEXT GENERATION. "Everybody in the cast is great and wonderful to work with," Spiner stated, "and it must be a nightmare for actors on other shows who don't get along because we all have to work 12 to 15 hours per day together."

Asked about the specific actors, Brent began, "It's an honor and pleasure to work with Patrick Stewart. He's the finest Shakespearean actor alive today. And Patrick tells us. . . " as he slips into an imitation of Stewart, "he's witty, intelligent, a real sex symbol, sophisticated, etc."

Regarding Marina Sirtis, Brent stated that she's, "The best Greek/British actress on television or theater." In describing LeVar Burton, he said, "A real prince of Africa who, when President of the U.S., will unite the nations of the world. Mr. Metaphysical!"

Gates McFadden, who had been forced out at the end of the first season, had just recently returned as the third season had only gotten under way a couple months before Spiner's convention appearance. "I'm really glad that she's back," Brent said enthusiastically. "She's gorgeous and it's wonderful to work with her again."

Then there's Michael Dorn. "All men on STAR TREK see themselves as sex symbols. Well, Michael really is one and certainly does have a way with women. In comparison, the first woman I had a serious love relationship with looked more like Vic Tayback."

The newest cast member at the time was also the best known, Whoopi Goldberg. "A great comedian," said Brent, "and terrific woman in every way."

Then there was the youngest cast member, Wil Wheaton. "We call him 'Cool Breeze' now. I used to be a 'Cool Breeze' once, when I was more his age. Now I'm just 'hot air.' "

And, of course, Jonathan Frakes, "A tremendous person and he gets bigger, nicer and more tremendous every year. Jonathan will be directing this year and we are really looking forward to it because we aren't allowed to give the directors a hard time, normally."

DUAL ROLES

Spiner was just getting warmed up and was clearly enjoying himself. "My most frequently asked question is if people can recognize me without my makeup. Let me ask, do you think you should recognize me in a grocery store or on the street?" To which a fan shouted out, "Only in spandex!" To which Brent quickly responded, "Oh good, because our third season uniforms aren't made of spandex any more."

Some of the questions were decidedly odd such as when he was asked whether Jonathan Frakes had any back or foot problems because the person asking believed that Frakes walked funny. "No," he replied, "he just walks like John Wayne," and Spiner demonstrated his swagger. "In fact, you may have noticed that when Jonathan sits in the command chair the backrest is straight up but Jonathan's body is way off to the side. It's amazing, isn't it? We don't know how he does it without falling out of the chair!"

Asked whether it was difficult playing the dual role in "Datalore," Brent stated that it wasn't hard to do, except technically. "Unfortunately, I was the guest star and they weren't even paying me. The hardest part was that I had to keep changing clothes 50 to 60 times per day because of the different camera angles required to film me at one angle as Data and then again in another as Lore for the same scenes."

LIFE BEFORE STAR TREK

When someone wondered if he could change anything in his professional or personal life, such as his appearance in the film RENT CONTROL, Brent chuckled and said, "RENT CONTROL was really a bad movie. I was glad I made it. It's an amazing credit to the producer, actually, because the movie was made on a budget of only $100,000 and looks like it must have cost more than $200,000. To answer your question, perhaps I wouldn't have done those couple episodes of MAMA'S FAMILY. I knew the director of NIGHT COURT and agreed to do MAMA'S in exchange for being on NIGHT COURT. Generally I felt I have been exactly where I wanted to be. I learned from the beginning of my career that I knew I had to suffer to be an actor. So I was prepared."

Regarding his experience on NIGHT COURT, Spiner recalled that, "It was great and easier to do than a STAR TREK episode because it was only a half-hour show. It would be rehearsed during the week, then filmed in front of a live audience on Fridays. I would love to do another one. In fact there has been a script waiting for two and a half years for me to do. I had gotten Paramount's permission to do it, too. I've never had the time to get around to it."

One of the other shows Spiner appeared in prior to THE NEXT GENERATION is THE TWILIGHT ZONE, and discussing the episode he was in he stated, "I consider TWILIGHT ZONE to be one of the greatest shows on TV. I was thrilled just to be a part of it."

COMIC MOMENTS

Only a blooper reel from the first season of THE NEXT GENERATION has been seen publicly and in it Brent Spiner is seen doing a George Bailey/Jimmy Stewart imitation while on the set of the Stargazer. When asked whether he's a fan of Jimmy Stewart, and if he does other imitations, Spiner stated, "Well, I really don't do a good enough job of imitating most of them, but Jimmy Stewart was one of my all time favorite

actors. I'd love to have him appear on TNG as a guest star, wouldn't you?" Whereupon Brent launched into a quit skit as Jimmy Stewart playing a Starfleet admiral. "And if you don't leave right now. . . we'll blast the holy hell out of you!" This was greeted by the audience with screams and applause.

Fans wanted to know whether the popular character "Q" would be back again and Spiner revealed, "John DeLancie is in an episode we're filming right now, 'Déjà Q,' " And this announcement was greeted with cheers, stomping and clapping. "Well, unfortunately he will be playing as Eugene." This brought cackles from people who knew that Eugene was the name of the character John DeLancie portrayed in many episodes of the soap opera DAYS OF OUR LIVES.

People wanted to know what his favorite episodes were, and Spiner said, "Actually you may be surprised but I really liked 'The Naked Now,' However, at the time the audience wasn't yet ready to see them break character because it was too early in the production to understand the characters as they were normally. I also liked 'Datalore' for obvious reasons. And I felt that 'Measure of a Man' was not just a good episode, but good television as well. Coincidentally, the actress who played the judge is from Texas. My first girlfriend was her roommate, so I've know her for years."

NAKED TIMES

The mention of Texas led to a fan from that state to ask Brent where he went to high school. "I went to Bel Air High School in Houston. It was a great school to go to if you wanted to be an actor. Harlan G. Andrews was the principal. He was the brother of the late actor Dana Andrews and looked just like him. You may have heard of Cecil Pickett, my acting teacher. I went to high school with Randy and Dennis Quaid, Cindy Pickett from ST. ELSEWHERE and Robert Wuhl from BATMAN. I went to probably 14 different colleges in all, foremost in my mind is the University of Houston and Trinity College in Dublin, Ireland. I even attended the famous Strassbourg Institute of New York. I haven't seen anyone I knew there getting any good acting work. But many people I went to high school with are doing plenty of acting, directing and producing for movies and TV."

Jonathan Frakes had revealed at another convention that he'd always wanted to play a trombone and finally got that opportunity in an episode of TNG, so when Brent Spiner was asked what he'd like to play if he got the chance, someone in the audience piped up with "Tasha Yar." Brent laughed and said, "Yes, Tasha Yar—definitely! Seriously, I've wanted to do about two or three thousand things on the show. But nothing in particular that I can think of at the moment. Perhaps the trombone as well, but I don't really know how to play it."

Back on the subject of "The Naked Now," someone asked why he put his elbow out and took a fall at the end of the scene. "That wasn't in the script at all. It was just something that I ad-libbed for fun, fully expecting it to be cut from the film. When they went to do the final editing, it had to be saved because they didn't have any other good takes and there wasn't enough time to do the scene over again. I was happy it made it into an episode because I liked how it turned out." And as to whether it was hard to do the drunk scene in that episode, the actor stated, "Acting drunk is the most difficult thing to play, especially if you don't drink. And of course I don't drink," he said, smirking and then looking innocent.

The episode "The Naked Now" includes the now famous sequence in which Tasha Yar seduces Data. When asked about this he said, "Well I certainly think Data and Tasha had something going! And I think that Tasha was more than a crush. I remember it vividly. After all, Data kept that holograph picture of her, didn't he? It's even in my hotel room tonight!"

INSIDE DATA

One of the questions people wondered about during the early seasons of THE NEXT GENERATION was whether Data would ever become human, which for a time seemed to be the android's goal. But Spiner stated that this would never happen. "No, Data is Pinocchio, just like Gene Roddenberry has envisioned him. Like any other character on the show he should grow and develop, too. This year he has not really reversed that development. It's time for the third season stories to develop other characters and ideas besides Data right now." In explaining Data and exactly how childlike the character is supposed to be, Spiner quipped, "I'd like to think that Data's character is the adult and Brent Spiner is the child."

Another popular episode which strongly features the character of the android is "Elementary Dear Data," and one fan wondered whether Brent was a fan of Sherlock Holmes and if he had any input on that particular episode?

"I have always loved Sherlock Holmes, especially Basil Rathbone, Chris Plumber, Frank Langella, and yes, (Jeremy) Brett, too, very much. And I was a big fan of the Chandler novels as a youth, too. So I was very excited to be playing a Sherlock Holmes character. But I had nothing to do with it being thought up or produced in an episode." As to whether the actors have any influence on the characters or storyline in a script, Brent explained, "Not a whole lot. Actors are just taking the initial direction that they want to go with the character. Directors aren't interested in our input. They are trying to look at the strengths of the actors and match that with the casting to come up with a finished product."

At another convention, Jonathan Frakes had remarked that Brent Spiner liked to play practical jokes, and when asked about this Brent replied, "When Jonathan doesn't know what to say, he lies. Actually there's not enough time [in the day's filming schedule] to set up any real practical jokes. However, it is a wild set full of comedians and everyone is on all the time.

Spiner was asked about whether Data is subject to the three laws of robotics created by Isaac Asimov, and

Brent responded that the android wasn't; that Data is controlled by Gene Roddenberry.

OUTSIDE DATA

A fan bluntly asked Brent if he wore a wig. "No, it's my very own hair. They dye it to darken it every day and slick it back. When Gene Roddenberry originally cast me as Data, he asked me if I would mind altering my appearance in some way. I told him, I can do that! Later Gene asked me if I'd be willing to shave my head. I told him, well, I guess I wouldn't be doing the part. So Gene had me go through something like 36 makeup tests, the colors ranging from battleship gray to bubble gum pink, including orange eyes. My makeup they finally selected is really bright gold, but the camera lighting cancels it out in some way."

This is also what he regards as the one drawback to playing the character. "The makeup is a drag to wear. It takes an hour and a quarter to put it on and twenty minutes to get it off. I can only get it off with kerosene. I've swallowed a lot of kerosene since I've begun this role. I asked Gene why a brilliant scientist like Noonian Sung, with the advanced technology of the time, couldn't have made Data with normal looking skin. Gene has a way of asking questions to make you see his way of thinking. GR asked, 'What makes you think that Data's skin isn't better?' Michael Westmore puts on the gold makeup personally for me every morning. Once when Michael didn't come in because he was home sick, another person did my makeup that morning. But when they began shooting, it didn't look right in the camera. So they called Michael in anyway to do it himself."

Someone wondered whether Spiner realized when he got the role that Data would become a character as popular as Spock was on the original series? At this he revealed, "When my agent got me the audition for STAR TREK: THE NEXT GENERATION, I was given all the character scripts to read. Having read the script for Data, I told them I was definitely interested in Data and auditioned for the part seven or eight times. I didn't anticipate that it would be the most popular character [he thanked the questioner for the comment], but I certainly thought it would be a nice character to play."

A VARIETY OF ROLES

As to what he looks for in a role, Spiner explained, "In the old days I took a part for the work and money. These days I only accept the parts whose characters are fun and humorous to me." Regarding any famous roles he might like to play he stated, "Yes, some Shakespearean roles. I once played Shylock in college, which is, oddly enough, one of Patrick Stewart's most famous Shakespearean roles. As a matter of fact, there's even a twisted bit of Shylock's dialogue from 'The Merchant of Venice' in 'The Naked Now.' ['If you prick me, do I not. . . leak?'] But I had nothing to do with it

being in the script."

On the subject of why he finally decided to make a convention appearance, he gave this as his reason. "A year of facing the demons in my life and things that scare me, and I finally decided to do it. You see there is no way to prepare for this. You have to be yourself. I guess it took me awhile to try it and I still wasn't prepared for this experience."

When it comes to acting, Spiner was asked if he preferred playing roles with dark humor in them such as he'd done on NIGHT COURT as well as in the movies MISS FIRECRACKER and RENT CONTROL. "I played in MISS FIRECRACKER because my best friend from high school, Tommy Schlamme, was the director. Trey Wilson from my high school is in it. I do like that style of humor."

Since Brent Spiner is an odd name, someone asked whether that was his real name. "Yes," he replied, "it's the name I was born with. I was named by my mother after the actor, George Brent, who in later years I discovered was really a very boring actor. When I mentioned it to my mother, she told me I was also a very boring child."

INSIDE STAR TREK

At this time the character of Lore had only appeared in "Datalore," but fans were wondering whether Data's evil twin would be returning. "Marina said I am closer in character to Lore than to Data. I'd like to see Lore come back. After all, he was just beamed out into space with a phaser weapon in his hand. He's probably wreaking havoc all over space by now." And of course Lore did return in season four in "Brothers."

Spiner revealed an interesting piece of information regarding the episode featuring Tasha Yar's funeral and her final message, which was played on the holodeck, and this is that she had a personal message for Data that said: "Data, it did happen." Regarding why the line was cut, he explained, "The producers decided to cut it from the episode because they didn't feel it was the right thing for Tasha to say. I don't know all their reasons for it, but I would have liked to have kept that part in the script."

The episode "Loud As A Whisper" was also special in that they worked with Howie Seago, a deaf actor. "That was a very educational experience for us all. The sound stage tends to get very loud at times and it can be distracting to all of the actors. But Howie couldn't hear any of that, so his focus was intense and concentrated at all times. His interpreter taught me sign, which was in ASL [American Sign Language] and Howie wanted it to be correct. But he was incredibly sensitive about every aspect of how it was done, including wanting the audience to see Data struggle with the translations so television viewers wouldn't assume that signing was extremely easy to learn or master. And he didn't want to discourage deaf viewers who might be struggling with ASL themselves."

Acting and learning lines isn't an easy thing to do as Spiner readily admitted. "If I really think about it, I really don't know how I manage to do it. Sometimes on Sunday night I look at the next week's script and as I run down the page I see what we've come to call 'Data Babble' and shake my head. But by rehearsal time, it just happens. I can't explain how or why."

This also had much to do with how Brent prepared himself emotionally for the scene in "Measure of a Man" when Riker tears off Data's arm. "Physically, well, we had Dr. Crusher standing by with a surgical team just in case. . . Emotionally, hmmm, I can't really put it into words."

After some joking around, the audience got Brent to discuss his favorite STAR TREK motion picture. "I'm a big fan of WRATH OF KHAN. The scene I love best is where William Shatner as Kirk is yelling, 'Kaaahhhnnnnn!' "

Brent revealed that even before his involvement with TNG he was interested in science fiction. "Yes, I read Asimov, Heinlein and particularly watched a lot of science fiction films."

At the time of this interview, which was two years into the series, Spiner was asked if there was one scene in the series he would want to be remembered for if the show suddenly disappeared. He thought about it for a moment and then said, "Naaah."

POST-PERFORMANCE IMPRESSIONS OF THE AUDIENCE

Brent Spiner had confessed to feeling very nervous as he stepped out on stage to take the microphone. But by the end of Saturday evening's performance it was clear that whatever demons Spiner had wrestled with were exorcised. Murmurs heard among departing spectators confirmed my own personal opinion. They were pleased and left feeling that they'd gotten their money's worth, considering this was Spiner's first convention experiment. Brent radiated a genuine feeling of warmth, sensitivity and caring towards the people in the audience.

He freely confessed self-consciousness about telling an audience about himself, rather than hiding it as an actor playing a role. I noticed that most of his answers to fan questions were thoughtful and honest. When he couldn't or wouldn't answer a question, he would make a joke as a retort. His "lounge act" was "real" comedy, not canned jokes.

Spiner's brief bursts into song were of decent vocal quality and purposefully done to illustrate points. Being an experienced con attendee, I wince when thinking about other STAR TREK guest stars who have included, as a filler for their acts, singing that was embarrassingly poor. At the conclusion he was grinning widely as he waved good-bye, thanked the wildly applauding audience, and made his hasty retreat off stage.

I have tried to be honest and objective in relating "just the facts." Now for my confession. . . I am such an avid Data fan that the vanity plate on my car reads "MRDATA." Okay? I was so thrilled to see Brent Spiner in person that my voluminous notes may have been a bit blurry from sweating palms and holding an unsteady pen. Hopefully this convention report has accurately given Brent Spiner the credit he is due. Data is my forever favorite character in the STAR TREK universe. Data has already stimulated an endless supply of story ideas for me as a new fiction writer. It's Brent Spiner's talented interpretation which has enabled a fictional android to become truly "alive" for us all. In my opinion, Data's character will remain freshly imaginative and uncontaminated by science fiction stereotypes so long as Spiner is minding the helm. Finally, the last word to describe Brent Spiner's appearance in New York is INTRIGUING!

CHAPTER 3

At the wedding of Marina Sirtis on June 21, 1992 we see Levar Burton, Michael Dorn, Patrick Stewart and Brent Spiner.

Photo credit: Albert Ortega, ©1993 Ron Galella Ltd.

Michael Dorn at the wedding of Marina Sirtis on June 21, 1992.

In January 1990, Michael Dorn, alias Lt. Worf, appeared at BASH CON in Massachusetts and spoke with his fans.

CHAPTER 3
MICHAEL DORN

By Diana Collins

Michael Dorn made his appearance at the Sheraton Tara Hotel in Braintree, Massachusetts at 3:00 p.m. on Saturday and Sunday afternoon. His talk was preceded by a STAR TREK parody called "Two Times Trek," which he commented upon very appreciatively when stepped out on stage. In the Tara Ballroom, a wildly cheering audience began to welcome the actor with a standing ovation. Dorn chuckled, made several appreciative gestures towards the onlookers and thanked the crowd.

He laughed, "That parody was pretty funny, wasn't it? Those players seemed to have sized up a lot of the quirks and problems on the show, haven't they? Anyway, I'd like to welcome you to the convention. Thanks for coming. Also, best wishes from the gang at Paramount for making our show as popular as it is.

"Actually we had a wonderful thing a little while ago where we were doing a scene, The Picard Maneuver. That's what we called it. We were all sitting around having a meeting and the camera shoots a big master, then shoots singles of all of us. And we all had lines, and after each one of us said our lines, Jonathan went, 'And Captain, I think that's what we should do,' and tugged on his uniform. Marina went next to give her lines and did it—in fact her uniform fits too tight to have anything to really tug on. So she had to pretend to grab the material to smooth it. When the next person tried saying the same line, he covered his mouth and mumbled, and everyone began laughing hysterically. It was hilarious.

"We've had a good time this year," Dorn continued. "Jonathan directed our 16th episode. It's the one about Data building a child. He always wanted a daughter so he built one, and it doesn't work. I gotta take some shots at him [Brent Spiner], you know?

"We're very happy with the new season and Worf has some wonderful stuff coming up. In fact the whole show has been doing pretty well. We're starting one in another week where he goes out to—oh, I can't tell you that. They'd kill me if I told you that." But the audience pleaded with him to tell.

"You know what they say? 'You know, Michael, we love that you go to these conventions and all of that, but you have a big mouth because everybody always knows what's going to happen.' Actually, Picard goes out to a pleasure planet loaded with women! Patrick Stewart has said, 'You know, Michael, I think this is a wonderful show. But Picard doesn't do anything! I want to go down to a planet with women and have a lot of gratuitous sex, ya know?'

"So I said, yeah, I think they'll write that for you. So he finally gets it." Not realizing what he said, Dorn is forced to pause when his pronouncement is met with hoots and hollers from the audience over his innocent innuendo. "You know, it's been a while since I've been to these conventions. I forgot how sick you people are," he cackled.

BEHIND THE SCENES

On the subject of the return of Dr. Crusher to the series in the third season, Dorn observed, "You know that Gates is back. They're kind of hard pressed to figure out where she was. They just sort of didn't do anything about that. They didn't write, well, that she was on vacation, she had a hernia operation or something. But all of a sudden she disappeared. Which is okay, but I gotta' tell you, I love Gates. Gates is really wonderful, but I like Diana [Muldaur]. She was really interesting. In fact she and Worf were going to have a little something going on, but she left before then."

Dorn had an interesting little revelation about Wil Wheaton. "Wesley is turning 18 this year. Actually the gang was all going to take him out for his 18th birthday but his mother pleaded with us not to, because Jonathan and I are silly people. Even Patrick's a nut! In fact at times we call him Captain Pecan, the wackiest nut in the galaxy." The audience groaned. "Hey! They write it for me, and I read it, okay?"

The questions Dorn was asked really ran the gamut, beginning with one which fastened on the idea that the actor could become just as strongly identified with Worf, even twenty years later, as Leonard Nimoy is with the character of Spock today. But Dorn didn't think that was likely in his case. "For some reason I just don't think that people are going to say, 'Oh, well, he reminds me too much of Worf.' I don't know if you noticed, but ahhh, I wear a lot of makeup!"

Regarding his makeup routine, Dorn explained how it starts each work day. "Actually I'm the first one there every morning, at 5:00 AM. I go through three separate stages. In the first stage they glue the cap on. Then I go to another chair and they glue the wig on and coif it. And this year they've had problems because I kind of look like Donna Reed. Prince Valiant is another character I'm compared to.

The poor hair-girl gets a little upset when we start singing the theme song from the DONNA REED SHOW. Then I go back to another chair for the beard and the Fu Manchu mustache and some little finish work, and then I get into wardrobe. And that's two hours, which is wild. When I get off late, I have just enough time to come home, throw some food down my throat and go to bed."

WORF THE WIMP?

Asked if he's a native of California, Dorn revealed that he is although he wasn't born there. "I was born in Texas but was raised in Pasadena, California, where the Rose Parade is. At this point in my life I hate Rose Parades. My aunt lived about four blocks from the parade route and every year we would park cars for a dollar fifty. 'Parking, parking, $1.50!' Then we'd go out to the parade route, sit on rocks and things. It wasn't the most comfortable situation."

Dorn was asked whether Worf would ever win a fight anywhere other than on the holodeck. This exposed a sore point that Dorn has had with the writers on the show. "Actually there is an episode where Riker and Worf fight, but I told Gene that I didn't want to get beat up any more. Last Year, or rather the year before, after the first season, I told him I love the character and I love doing it. However, Worf gets beat up by everybody on the show. It's like this thing on the Enterprise. The Captain and Worf meet some new guy in the Transporter room. No matter what he is or who he is, the Captain will say, 'Hello, I'm Captain of the Enterprise and this is Mr. Worf. Would you like to beat up on him? Go ahead. And Mr. Worf, let them win, too.' It got to the point where it was just ridiculous. So he said that he wanted to show that whoever was doing the beating up was so powerful that he could beat up Worf; that he could beat up anybody. But he got a little ridiculous with the old commander or the old admiral who could do it, you know what I mean? It was just awful.

"As it turns out, he said he'll stop that and I said thank you because it is a little disgusting. He got beat up again this year, too, from the guy in 'The Hunted.' Wasn't that guy good? I don't know if you guys have seen much theater, but he was in Les Miserables and he played the police officer. Really good guy, beautiful voice, and did a really wonderful job. That reminds me of something we were talking about [during 'The Hunted']. For some, Marina has all these affairs with these great looking guys. She's walking down the hall, miles away from this guy, and she goes, 'There's a cute guy in there.' I said to her, where? I mean, I couldn't believe her! Marina, she is this crazed. It's like radar."

INSIDE AND OUTSIDE STAR TREK

Dorn discussed his work in the theater, and stated, "I did about three or four plays in L.A. before I started in the business. That's what I started out to do, to be a stage actor, and this is how it just turned out. My favorite is 'Cat On A Hot Tin Roof.' I played the Elizabeth Taylor role." That's a joke, son! "Actually not this year, but next year some of the cast are going to try and get together to do a stage play because we're all classically trained and we love doing that."

Regarding how Dorn landed the role of Worf, one person stated that they'd heard that he auditioned for the part by acting obnoxious and pushy. "Was I obnoxious? Well, yeah, I was a bit aloof and standoffish, and not very nice to the secretaries and the producers. I mean, I was polite but I just wasn't like (in a sweet voice) 'Hi!' when I met them. When I walked into the interview, people just said nicely, 'Well, hi—Mr. Dorn, is it?' And I would say, 'Yes.' Then the secretaries said, 'Would you like to have the signs to read?' (Michael sternly polite) 'Thank you. Do you have a room where I can be by myself?' The secretary in surprise says, 'Yeah, sure. Over there.' And I met the producers and I would just go (polite, stern voice), 'Hi, Michael Dorn. Pleasure to meet you,' down the row of producers sitting at the table. That was it. And I read and then said, 'Thank you very much.' One of the producers told me they thought I was psycho. So that's why they hired me."

When asked why he thought that THE NEXT GENERATION had less gratuitous violence in it than the original series did, Dorn remarked, "I thought there should be more violence [in the 24th century], actually. But I've got to admit that I was wrong.

Whenever Gene explained his views of the future to me, whenever he talked to people about this, his view of the universe is a little more placid. Instead of killing anything that's just different than you are—you know, I'd be dead if that were the case. 'Worf, you're different. Die!' He just thought that the galaxy would be a more peaceful place.

"The Enterprise is not a warship," Dorn stressed. "It's a starship. It's an exploratory ship. That's what he believes, and it works because we have a lot of the original fans that like our show, plus a lot of new fans that really never watched STAR TREK before, and people that just like good TV."

STAR TREK RITUALS

Dorn was asked about a scene in which Worf was describing a Klingon ritual involving hurling heavy objects and clawing, whereupon Worf was seen to lick his teeth.

"I didn't do that, did I?" Dorn wondered. "They really didn't have any idea about it, they just wrote it. They just said that Worf describes this and just gave me the lines and that's it. It was really my idea to just go off in this haze. Actually Patrick really liked that. He said that was pretty funny. He and his wife, Sheila, were on the floor. It just made sense to me. He's describing it as so intense that he started going (in Worf's voice) 'They scream at you and hurl heavy objects.' And I don't remember licking my teeth. What an actor, ya' know?"

On the subject of how long it takes to shoot an episode and the average production costs, Dorn explained, "It takes about seven actual working days. We work from about 12 to 14 hours a day and we have about the biggest budget, not only in syndicated TV—we have the biggest budget in TV. Our budget is about 1.5 million dollars per episode. But believe me, Paramount's going to get it all back when they go into major syndication, because you have to have 100 and something episodes for major syndication. It's going to start going all over the world, and believe me, it's going to be worth the money."

Then there's the number of aliens in the show and whether viewers would be seeing delegations and ambassadors from other planets. Regarding this aspect of the series Dorn stated, "Yes, they have already. They have fish people. Do you believe that? Fish! Did you know that one of them was (in Worf's tone) 'What a handsome race!' Worf is a sick person. They're going to bring more and more aliens into the episodes. Did you know that the head fish, the leader, was Mick Fleetwood from Fleetwood Mac? He wanted to do the show badly then, and now he doesn't ever want to do it again. When we were talking to Mick initially, he was going, 'Yeah, like this is great! This is great!' After he got in makeup he talked like this," and Dorn made garbled sounds in a very stiff lipped manner.

Dorn revealed that, at that time, his favorite episode was one of the early Klingon oriented storylines, "Matter of Honor." "I'd say my favorite episode was where Riker goes over in the Officer's Exchange Program because it really does show that Klingons have a sense of humor."

Worf's costume was changed after the first season and regarding that Dorn said, "The cloth, the first year, was sort of like a throwback to the original sash, which they dug out of Paramount wardrobe. It was nice, and it was light. It was kind of a little thing. But they got the idea the second year and said, oh, Michael, it's nice but we'd like it to be a little more macho—heavier. So they started making this thing out of aluminum rings and leather—stuff like that, and it weighed ten pounds! And I was going, yeah, this is real great. And that's another point for people who joke about me. One guy throws in that it looks like he's wearing a lot of beer can tops today, but they wanted it to be a little heavier and more macho. Personally I don't like it. I liked the other one much better."

At the time of this convention there were rumors that Brent Spiner and Michael Dorn were leaving the series, to which Dorn quickly responded, "Oh God, no. Brent and I just bought houses this year and we gotta pay for those babies! It was right around Christmas when we were with Gene and told him that we'd just bought houses and Gene goes to the others, 'We got 'em.' Actually our contract is for three more years."

A background question about Worf concerned whether the Klingon, who was raised by human foster parents, had any special schooling in order to study his Klingon heritage. "Well I don't think he took Klingon 101 or anything," Dorn quipped. "But in the 24th century the writers thought that Worf, because he is so proud of his race, would learn as much as he can. And with computers the way they are in the 24th century, you can dig up anything you want."

THE TRUTH ABOUT WORF

Since "Q" has become a popular character, Dorn was asked about the return of that arrogant alien. "Yes, in two weeks. I hate that guy. You can't grab him and if you try to take him to the brig, he may turn you into a table. It's a good episode, too. I mean, we really scream and fight with these guys [the writers] to have good stories and to really do characters well. I have to admit they do a wonderful job."

In the episode in which there was a Klingon hand-sniffing sex scene, Dorn was asked whether that was his idea? "No. They figured that these two are animals, first of all. It's sort of like you just get into it and a lot of the crew was starting to giggle. But what I did was a little extra."

Questioned about the future and where he'd like to see his career go after THE NEXT GENERATION, Dorn stated, "I want it to go up! Down is bad. Up is good. Actually STAR TREK is a wonderful vehicle. Most of the roles I've done in the past have been good-guy roles, and my manager and I were actively looking for roles that would show me in kind of a bad light. Sort of a tough guy."

When someone piped up that they remembered Dorn in CHIPS, he replied, "Yeah, nice guy, huh?" Then the actor went into a routine in a sweet voice mimicking the character he played. " 'You went too fast, sir. Here's a ticket. . . and drop that gun!' and the bad guy says complacently, 'Oh, he's too nice. I won't shoot him.' The problem is, that kind of role limits your career. So we were actively looking for roles that were mean, sort of nasty and psycho and look who came along!

"I have a funny story about when I was with this guy in New York. I was talking about my past and what I had done before. I've done all these roles and one that I've always done that I just don't want to do any more is cops, so I'm glad that I got in STAR TREK,. I don't want to play cops. That's all I've been in my life are cops, cops, cops! I'm so glad that's over. The guy looked over at me. He said, 'Uh, Michael, uh. . . you're head of security, right?' And I said yeah. 'You're still a cop.' And I went, no, uh, but uh. . . And all of a sudden I got distraught. I'm a cop. Anyway, I'm glad I got a role that's a little more anti-social."

MICHAEL DORN— STAR TREK FAN

When asked whether he misses Tasha Yar, who was played by Denise

Crosby, he replied, "Not by Worf. He got her job. Actually we miss her, but the problem is that we didn't want to do anything, because she wanted out. I mean, really bad. She was unhappy because she wasn't getting a lot to do by herself. But it's tough. We've got nine regulars on the show and it's really tough to feature one person every show. She was very unhappy about that and she really wanted to get out. She got along really well and came back for an episode which was wonderful. Dorn was referring, of course, to "Yesterday's Enterprise."

Dorn is a big fan of Trek Classic and says his favorite episode is "Elaan of Troyius." "The one with France Nuyen, the dolman." Dorn whistles. "Hot tamale!" Asked if he's met any of the original STAR TREK stars he said, "Yes, I met George Takei. He told me it's not pronounced 'tak-eye,' it's pronounced 'te-kay.' And I've met Walter Koenig, Nichelle Nichols and Jimmy Doohan. He and I did a couple of game shows together." But he hadn't yet met William Shatner at that time as it would be a couple years before Dorn appeared in STAR TREK VI—THE UNDISCOVERED COUNTRY. "I haven't met him or Spock. But DeForest Kelley did the first episode, which was nice."

A great many STAR TREK novels have been written over the years and Dorn stated that he has read some of them. "They're very good. Actually the cast collectively think that these guys should be writing for us. ST—TNG is an hour movie that we are doing. With the budget that we have

and the caliber of people behind us behind the camera. But in an hour movie it's tough to get everything in. It's almost impossible. The best thing to do is just to leave the things hanging that perhaps we can pick up later. Or like the writers said, they're going to have to deal with it on their own."

LIFE ON THE SET

Since the scenes from a TV show or a movie are filmed out of order, he was asked whether this made it difficult for Dorn to deal with the continuity of a story as it applied to his character? "It would seem difficult to do that, to do the beginning of the show at the end or do the end of the show at the very beginning and be able to know where you're going. It's very simple. You just read the script. But it does get difficult with the [amount of] time because they're getting scripts to us like the day before the shoot. We've been screaming about that for the past two years. And it is especially hard for Brent because he has a lot of dialogue. It's very tough, but he is funny. He said if you're going to do that, I want cue cards. He won't ever use them. He just has them write them up to bug them."

There was an episode where Data had a beard at the beginning, an obvious reference to William Riker. The same episode also had a scene shot at the end where Data appeared to be bald, a reference to Captain Picard. Dorn confirmed that the scene was indeed planned. "Well, it was written, but it didn't come off. It came very close, though. I think the day before it was to be filmed they said, 'Nahh. That's in bad taste.' "

Regarding acting schedules and whether they allow him to do outside work during the normal season, Dorn said, "With our schedule, no. It's pretty tough because you have to get out there and read for the roles at times. Like I said, it's good to be working and we should just thank God that we're doing it. When it finally does come to a close, then we'll go on."

QUALITY CONTROL

At this time no two-part episodes had been done yet beyond the original two hour pilot, "Encounter At Farpoint," and Dorn agreed that he did think they should do some more. "Yeah, we've been yelling at them to do that, too. They should, it just lends itself. Picard leaves the planet and goes, 'Well, that's your problem. We're just going back to the ship.' What they do is they leave cliffhangers at times. The show about my brother and I is going to be a cliffhanger because that's not going to be resolved. Now there's going to be a lot of things unresolved and for some reason they just don't feel that it's necessary. That's their business. Most of our writers get to the end and say, 'How shall we end this? I can't think of anything.' 'I don't know either.' 'Let's go have lunch.' " Clearly Michael Dorn had some misgivings about some of the scripts, which he went on to explain.

"There was one show where Picard has just saved the people of the planet, and they're talking to him afterward. 'You did it. You saved us. How did you do it?' And he doesn't know. It just happened. He doesn't know if it was Q or something like that. So he says, 'Well, we'll get back to you.' He gets in his chair and says, 'Okay, let's get out of here!' And in the meantime he leaves the guy, like, on the phone! Then we're thinking, now wait a minute. Why don't we answer the guy? We'll have to explain things and that's not going to be easy, so why don't we just get the hell out of here."

Dorn also discussed the fact that most of the uniforms had changed that season. "A lot of it has changed because it's the Captain's prerogative. Patrick said that he hated the old uniform. Of course, you thought they were sexy. But we walk around like. . . (demonstrating a stiff, painful gait). And when he changed his uniform, everybody had to follow suit because he's the Captain. How do I get out of mine, I don't know. That wardrobe person zips me up in the back. In a way it's a shame because the fans that are making their own uniforms come up and say, 'Hey how do you like my. . . ooooh no.' "

STAR TREK DETAILS

Occasional questions dealt with Worf's background, such as whether the character minded being the only Klingon in a Federation job. "Worf doesn't mind too much because it's a higher minimum wage! The thing is, whatever you do as a soldier is what they're saying is important. During the first year of the show, one of my

Klingon cohorts said that to be able to live in this Federation environment is a triumph in itself. And property is cheap in the Federation. Worf is going to go into real estate. Sorry, I'm being silly here."

When asked about what he would like to see in a STAR TREK: THE NEXT GENERATION movie, Dorn managed to also go on to predict what would actually happen in a forthcoming two part episode. "Umm, Klingon lovemaking. Actually what I think is the Borgs, to finally get a look at their home planet, where they're from; the whole thing. And have a running battle with them for two episodes," which of course happened in "The Best of Both Worlds." The Klingon lovemaking and Borg homeworld visit remain unrealized at the moment, though.

Dorn also had an interesting revelation about the character of Geordi LaForge when someone asked if Geordi was ever going to get his normal sight back. "You know, he's been trying to get rid of those VISORs for three years, and he wants to. But I don't know if they're ever going to let him do it. Of course that would make him much different. But you gotta think, in the 24th century, couldn't they just take care of it? It just always kills me that when he's in a fight or something, he always loses his VISOR. Then he picks up a rock or anything and bangs it into his head and says, 'No, that's not it. Don't mind me. I'm just bitter.' "

DETAILS, DETAILS. . .

Brent Spiner was on the TONIGHT SHOW once and remarked that he and Dorn received a lot of marriage proposals. While Dorn said that he doesn't receive a lot, there was one that concerned him. "The one fan letter I'm concerned about was this one lady who thought that Worf was very sexy and she wanted to have his love child. I just figured that anybody that thought that Worf was great father material. . . that's when I moved."

During the first season a subplot was introduced wherein Wesley was going to be left in the care of Worf, who would have to both train the boy in self-defense as well as tuck him in at night. "You never know what's going on in these people's [writers] heads. The tucking in bed thing was an interesting proposition, and they may touch on it this year. It just hasn't panned out so far."

Asked how he keeps physically fit, Dorn said that he concentrates on keeping in shape during the off season, which is the three month hiatus between seasons. "That's when I go and really pump iron and sort of get in shape for the next year. Because you've got only that amount of time to do it. But you just balance it by eating the right foods, like candy and donuts, five or six cups of coffee a day with lots of sugar, ice cream at night. . . late."

Dorn revealed how the long hours working on a TV series affects his family life, "Well, they left me a little while ago and. . . gosh, I'm just kidding. I'm not married. I'm a bachelor. So on weekends it's heeeaaaaa! Actually it's worked out well because we actors bitch and moan about not working when we don't have jobs. And then when we start working we say, 'Oh, we work so hard!' But I don't complain."

Dorn had an interesting reply when asked whether it was difficult working with the special visual effects which are added later which require him to act against nothing in the original scene. "No, we call it face acting. You do that with any show. You're a certain character and you're supposed to do a certain thing. It's very simple."

SUMMING UP

Michael Dorn looked happy and relaxed during his entire performance in his black sweater, shoes and slacks, completed by a black and silver tweed jacket. More than a few surprised and appreciative faces lit up as Dorn appeared on stage. Spectators could verify with their own eyes that there was a "foxy looking" human hidden beneath that "turtlehead" appliance and Klingon makeup worn for the ST—TNG series.

I had heard rave reviews about his appearances from other convention goers, so I was prepared to be entertained. But I was very impressed by Michael Dorn's down to earth warmth and "big teddy bear" personality. His appreciation for fans clearly came through by the way he described all of the behind the scenes

events with the ST—TNG cast and production crew. Dorn is also very talented in the art of verbal fencing with crowds during the question and answer session. When I managed to personally talk to him about this after the show, his comment was, "I'm just a big ham."

As to the test of whether the audience got their money's worth? Besides the standing ovations and the boisterous applause interspersed throughout his speech, most of the 400+ Trekkers lined up to get his autograph. Michael Dorn graciously signed autographs for every single fan who stood in line and briefly chatted with each of them, which took several minutes longer than the "one hour only" commitment in the BASH CON schedule. He passed my test with flying colors.

CHAPTER 4

Levar Burton at the education First Week Honors CBS Entertainment Ceremony held on Dec. 4, 1992.

Photo credit: ©1993 Ron Galella Ltd.Levar Burton

Levar Burton and Brent Spiner, together offstage as well as on,
at the TNG Tribute of the Museum of Radio and TV held on March 14, 1992.

Like Brent Spiner, LeVar Burton was initially reluctant to make any public appearances at STAR TREK conventions. But he finally gave in and appeared at the OCTOBER TREK, held October 4-6, 1991.

CHAPTER 4
LEVAR BURTON SPEAKS

By Diana Collins

"The reason I'm here," Burton began, "is because I figure that I held out long enough; it's time to get wet. I want to share with you some of my thoughts and feelings about the show. This industry of TV is a way of educating and enlightening as well as entertaining. STAR TREK is a major teaching tool. I sit on the fringe in this group. I believe there are many people in other galaxies that are watching STAR TREK and us, preparing us for the future eventuality of being out there in the stars. This is one of the most powerful ways to face ourselves, through going out to the stars and seeing other aliens through ourselves." Burton said he talked with Jonathan Frakes about what to expect at a convention and his co-star assured him that he could expect a warm reception.

"STAR TREK: THE NEXT GENERATION: It's not just an adventure, but it's what I feel I came here to do in this life."

On the show it has been established that Geordi and Data are best friends. But life can imitate art as this relationship continues off camera as well. "Brent and I hang out a lot together," LeVar stated. "Brent's one of the smartest people breathing on the planet. He possesses a wit that is classically funny and has one of the highest IQ's I've ever known. He has a remarkable gift for being able to be honestly funny all of the time."

The episode "Elementary Dear Data" featured Data and Geordi in the roles of Holmes and Watson on the holodeck, but because of a problem they encountered, the pair probably won't repeat those classic roles. "The Sherlock Holmes episode was a lot of fun to do. Unfortunately the estate of Sir Arthur Conan Doyle complained to the studio for not asking permission to use his character. I guess it's their job to protect the Sherlock Holmes image. So it's unlikely that we'll be able to do it again." In spite of all that, Dr. Moriarty did make a return appearance in year six of THE NEXT GENERATION. This may well be because Moriarty appeared in only one of Doyle's original stories and that one has long been in the public domain.

CAREER AND CHARACTER DIRECTIONS

Inevitably the performers are asked about how they landed their popular role on THE NEXT GENERATION, although in LeVar's case he was also asked how he felt when he auditioned for the part. This is an interesting question because LeVar Burton had gained a lot of attention in 1977 in the TV mini-series ROOTS, but his career had done a slow fade thereafter.

"I had come to the point in my life where I was ready for anything," LeVar stated candidly. "So I went there and gave it my best shot. I had a problem at first understanding the role

of a blind officer. I tried to act blind while auditioning. The producers took me aside and told me about the VISOR device which allows Geordi to see like anyone else. Then I read the dialogue again with this in mind and apparently they liked the job I did."

The one person Burton said is responsible for his having the opportunity to land the role is producer Bob Justman. "He produced a show a long, long time ago called EMERGENCY which Gary Lockwood and I starred in. So when STAR TREK: THE NEXT GENERATION was being cast, Bob brought up my name and demanded that I be given an audition because he thought I'd be great on the show."

Early in the series, Brent Spiner and LeVar Burton conceived the idea that Geordi and Data would have a special bond and form a team called The Perceivers. "The name was to indicate that they could both 'see' things exactly as they were because I had my VISOR and Data had his computer-like brain. Of course, the writers abandoned the idea immediately. I feel the relationship has continued and that they are very close. I'd like to have moments of character relationship developed for Geordi in general, too. I think we'll meet someone from his past and maybe his family in the future."

Burton also wants to see Geordi's private life get some more exposure. "I went to Rick Berman and asked that Geordi finally get his sexuality explored. After all, we've explored the sexuality of everyone else, including the android." As to how Geordi's character differs from the rest of the crew, he said, "Geordi is probably more satisfied with himself. He is the loosest member of the crew. He doesn't take things as seriously. Picard especially doesn't have enough fun in his life compared to Geordi."

BURTON AND GOLDBERG

LeVar Burton's outside activities include being the voice of Captain Planet. "Whoopi Goldberg is the voice of another character in that show, too. Brent Spiner and I together have created another TV show called UNDERCOVERS which is half live action, half animation. We've sent the idea to the networks. I hope we'll see it on TV some day."

Burton revealed that he had a hand in Whoopi Goldberg joining the cast of NEXT GENERATION. "I happened to talk to Whoopi during the hiatus between the second and third season. I told the staff and they thought I was crazy or making a joke until she contacted them herself. Then they finally believed me! Whoopi's a real fan of STAR TREK and she was seriously interested in being on the show in some way. The writers were just then expanding the show with a Ten-Forward Lounge. Her interest in playing a minor character inspired them to place her in a semi-regular hostess/bartender role. It was a perfect fit. And don't you love her costumes and those hats? We affectionately call her shuttle-head for the hat."

On the subject of Guinan,

Burton was asked whether her background is going to ever be revealed since so little is known about the character.

"I don't know how much they intend to reveal, but there's a wonderful mystique that has been developed concerning Guinan. The writers try to keep us separated from the script writing staff, but they do want to keep that mystique in her character."

The Borg have proven to be popular adversaries on the series and LeVar Burton revealed that he has some ideas of his own about these characters which he'd like to see come about. "I'd like to see them return and I have a good storyline for a ST—TNG feature film that I'm working on now."

READING RAINBOW AND SPACE CAMP

Since Patrick Stewart and Jonathan Frakes have directed episodes of THE NEXT GENERATION, one would think that perhaps LeVar Burton might be interested in expanding his talents in that direction as well. But at the time of this appearance, in October of 1991, he expressed no interest in directing.

"No, I'm focusing all of my free time, if there is such a thing, into my own Eagle Nation Films Company. I'm putting all of my energy into its upcoming project films. I think Jonathan and Patrick are excellent directors because they know the language of actors and how to lead the

NEXT GENERATION

cast like generals." Burton would gradually come around and a year and a half later he would direct the outstanding sixth season entry "Second Chances."

One of Burton's outside activities involves being the host of the PBS children's show READING RAINBOW. As to how he got involved in a program like this, the actor revealed, "My mother was an English teacher. I grew up learning that reading was an example of normal human beings. Since today kids see so much TV, this was the perfect medium to catch their interest. We spent the first two years on the show feeling as if we were carrying rocks uphill, trying to get kids, and everyone else, to notice the show."

Of the books he'd read on the show up to that time, his favorites were THE LEGEND OF THE INDIAN PAINT BRUSH, THE GIFT OF THE SACRED DOG and HILL OF FIRE. But it was difficult at first to get the show going. "A book has to lend itself to TV by being exciting enough and educational enough to show. During our first few seasons we had to beg publishers to give us books to put on the air. Today those publishers unashamedly court the READING RAINBOW producers."

When asked if Space Camp is truly as educational as he made it appear in an episode of READING RAINBOW, Burton praised it with great enthusiasm. "It's an unbelievable educational experience! Wouldn't it be great if the U.S. government funneled everything from the defense budget into the space program?" The suggestion was greeted with a roar of applause.

Asked if the actor would like to do a Space Camp spin-off to show all of the positive things we have in our lives today due to the accomplishments of the space program, Burton stated, "Yes, that would be wonderful and might inspire us to get back into space. There are so many practical inventions in science, medicine, technology, engineering— every field. One example of a device which contributes to our welfare in our daily lives is a fireman's suit. There are so many advances we've made due to space exploration!" And when asked if he'd go on a space shuttle should he ever be invited, Burton unhesitatingly replied, "I'd snap up the opportunity to go in space in a second!"

SECRETS OF THE VISOR

It has been frequently pointed out that Geordi's VISOR is actually based on a hair barrette. When asked if he felt weird wearing a barrette on his face, LeVar dealt more directly with the problems associated with wearing something which covered his eyes.

"For the first two years I felt 'handicapped' as an actor by having to wear my VISOR. First, when it's positioned over my eyes, eighty percent of my normal vision is lost! It took away so much of my sight that I was always bumping into things on the set. Second, because the barrette covered part of my face, subtle expressions didn't come through very well on

44

camera. I had to learn to compensate by using more pronounced facial expressions with the parts of my face which were seen around the VISOR, and by using more dynamic body language to get the messages across. As a result, I feel I've become a better actor. I'm much more aware of exactly what my physical body is doing while acting."

Burton explained that it was Gene Roddenberry's idea to have a physically challenged character who could be a full contributor in the 24th century.

"He said to the writers, 'Let's have the blind guy fly the ship!' The VISOR barrette is attached to my head by an elastic band. Someone from wardrobe has to secure it, then tuck it under my hair to hide it. During the hiatus, our technical staff developed a prototype for a new VISOR. It looks essentially the same, but it screws into my head at the temples. This one should be easier to take on and off. The trick will be if I can do the show all day without getting a migraine headache from the pressure on my temples."

It's not any better when he removes the VISOR on camera, either, and the audience can see his supposedly blind eyes. "I'm wearing white opaque contacts and see nothing at all in them." And yet Burton doesn't feel that his character should get his normal eyesight restored. "If Geordi had normal eyesight, he'd be giving up a lot because he sees much more than a normal sighted person. It would be like giving a part of himself away."

Which is why the character turned down the chance to have his sight restored in an early episode. "Geordi felt satisfied with himself." Regarding Burton's personal view of the character he plays, he stated, "He's a warrior of sorts because he doesn't accept his limitations."

But just because the series is set in the 24th century, doesn't mean that the technology used to power the VISOR is exactly futuristic. "There's a transistor battery in a pack under my armpit with a wire attached which runs up to the back of my head and under my hair."

A VARIETY OF INTERESTS

Another difficulty in playing the roll of Geordi LaForge is learning the unusual technical jargon used in the 24th century.

"It's what we call techno-babble. The key is to believe what you say and talk as fast as you possibly can. Mike Okuda and the other technical guys lend a lot of credibility and consistency to the futuristic technical ideas because they are technical experts."

On an unrelated subject, LeVar Burton appeared in an infomercial for Anthony Robins "Building Unlimited Powers" program, and he was asked about this. The infomercial showed people doing fire walking and other similar feats of physical prowess.

"Tony Robins is an old friend of mine," Burton explained. "I did it to be supportive of him, not really as an endorsement of the product. I do strongly believe in the ability of human beings to access the total power from within."

Speaking of the power within, LeVar Burton had to summon up a great deal of patience when it came time to go under the makeup as a lizard-creature in the episode "Identity Crisis."

"It took seven hours and five makeup artists working on me at once," the actor revealed. "I spent fifteen hours per day in that makeup doing that episode. The artists built up these veins on top of my body suit, then painted ultraviolet sensitive paint on just the veins to create the glowing lizard effect. It was quite an ordeal and was hot inside the outfit. But my beloved, Stephanie Kozart, is one of the makeup artists, and that made it more enjoyable."

On the subject of hobbies, Burton explained that he doesn't need hobbies because he's having the time of his life doing what he does every day on THE NEXT GENERATION and with other performing work. But acting was always his goal in life. At one time he was studying to be a priest. "Yes, but I got to a certain point in my life where I realized I didn't want to be a priest any more."

On Beards and Bad Films

On a less profound level, Burton was asked if he ever tried to grow a beard. "Yes, I grew a beard during the hiatus. Rick Berman liked it. They were worried that it would cover up too much of my face, and the VISOR already covers up so much that I have

to compensate for it. So Rick did some test beard shots and it didn't get approved. Then I grew a beard during Christmas vacation again but had to shave it off in January. Oh well."

Asked about his background, the actor stated that he was born in West Germany. "My father was a photographer in the military and we moved around with his job. But I spent most of my growing up years in Sacramento, California."

Actors tend to have to do many things in order to keep food on the table, as well as to keep their careers alive, and Burton willingly admits this, such as when he was asked what the worst films or TV shows were that he's worked on.

"I had the honor of working with Nichelle Nichols on the worst show; that was called THE SUPERNATURALS," he stated. One should understand that among industry professionals, any project, whether movie or TV episode, is referred to as a 'show.' "Another bad one was a FANTASY ISLAND episode where Sammy Davis Jr. played my father. I was on a TRAPPER JOHN episode that wasn't that wonderful. But my second worst show was probably MIDNIGHT HOUR where I had the pleasure of working with Harry Belafonte."

When LeVar Burton tried out for THE NEXT GENERATION, he was well aware of what STAR TREK was all about.

"Like Whoopi, I saw myself represented in a future where races and genders worked together and made capable leaders. Unlike other futuristic shows which depicted no other races or women, STAR TREK offered a bright outlook that inspired me at a young age."

QUESTIONS ABOUT THE FUTURE

Burton admits that his strong opinions about the space program include a belief in life on other worlds. "It would be very egotistical to not believe in life on other planets!" Burton insisted. "And I hope that the innate goodness in human beings would come through so that we would make a good showing, should a 'first contact' opportunity arise."

Being out in public in front of an audience of hardcore fans at a convention means exposing oneself to a certain degree, and the sort of questions asked are limited only by the person asking them, which leaves a lot of room for wild cards to emerge, such as when someone asked LeVar what kind of contraceptives he thought the crew used in the 24th century?

"The condom endures!" he replied without hesitation. "Why fix it if it ain't broke?"

On to more prosaic subjects, the often asked question regarding how the Transporter effect is accomplished came up next. "The effect is created by the film crew shooting the Transporter scene twice," Burton patiently explained. "During the first shot they raise the lights while we hold still in our positions on the Transporter pad for a count of eight seconds. Then it's filmed once again while they lower the lights and we again hold still to a count of eight. Finally a special effects person stirs up a bowl of water filled with sparkles in front of the film and they put the two superimposed patterns together."

How hot is it on the Enterprise? someone asked. Although it wasn't made clear whether this was referring to the fictional Enterprise or the standing sets inside the Paramount sound stages, Burton replied, "It's always 68 degrees, unless life support malfunctions, of course." And when asked what the dilithium crystals shown on THE NEXT GENERATION really were, he answered, "Very large chunks of common quartz crystal."

ON THE PERSONAL SIDE

Personal questions continued to crop up now and then, primarily on the prosaic side, such as whether or not Burton had any pets. "I had a German shepherd named Mozart who had been my pal since I was six years old," he sadly related. "He developed a degenerative condition which caused him to eventually lose all the feeling in his legs. It really wrecked me when I had to put him to sleep a year ago. I haven't been able to bring myself to get another dog. Stephanie has a cat and a bird that get along pretty well, and we're all getting ready to move into our new house!"

Regarding who his favorite bad guy is, Burton got political for the only time at this 1991 convention when he said, "George Bush, for what his administration is doing to this country, especially to our educational system. On STAR TREK: THE NEXT GENERATION it would be the creature Armus who killed Tasha Yar and slimed Commander Riker."

LeVar Burton appeared at this convention just a couple weeks before Gene Roddenberry died. When asked about Roddenberry's then current involvement with THE NEXT GENERATION, the actor said, "Given the choice, he'd be on the STAR TREK: THE NEXT GENERATION set every day. He keeps in touch by writing notes on the scripts and making phone calls from home to the production folks."

Asked to explain Roddenberry's interpretation of the universe of THE NEXT GENERATION, Burton stated, "Gene wants the conflict resolved in the 24th century in as non-violent a way as possible. It doesn't mean that there's no violence. But the crew, other than minor personality quirks, have evolved to the point where they get along well together. The conflicts occur when dealing with other/new races. Gene maintains that conflict in the future will be approached with a mature, humane, and intellectual attitude. We will choose not to shoot it out as warring opponents to resolve conflicts."

During his appearance, LeVar Burton was a dynamic, high energy speaker having fun while working the crowd. He answered the audience's questions graciously and politely. Mostly, I noticed that he was a soft touch when it came to kids and teachers with special requests.

I was delighted that LeVar had chosen to openly share some of his personal beliefs with us. His ideas about the power of the mind to improve human potential were inspiring. Mr. Burton's reflections that our space journeys will help us to understand ourselves better, were right on the mark. His idea that we can stretch the boundaries of the imagination until they become reality, is the very heart of science fiction. LeVar's belief that humanity possesses an innate goodness that will continue to guide our future is what STAR TREK is all about. Perhaps it's why he feels that STAR TREK is an excellent teaching tool and why he's so excited to be a part of this positive phenomena. I left the convention satisfied that I'd gotten my money's worth. . . and itching to go to Space Camp!

CHAPTER 5

John De Lancie arrives at Forest Lawn for Gene Roddenberry's memorial service on Nov. 1, 1991.

Photo credit: Albert Ortega, ©1991 Ron Galella Ltd.

A 1984, pre-Next Generation shot of John De Lancie with his then-pregnant wife.

He's made more reappearances on STAR TREK: THE NEXT GENERATION than any other guest star. John De Lancie made his first appearance as "Q" in the very first episode of TNG and has been a recurring surprise visitor almost every season since. But this is an actor who has a lot of interesting things to say, and they don't all have to do with STAR TREK.

CHAPTER 5

JOHN DE LANCIE: THE HUMAN SIDE

By Diana Collins

The large Rockville, Maryland audience rose to applaud John De Lancie as he made his entrance at August 15, 1992 TREKON. De Lancie paced across the stage, speaking with an intense eloquence. It was easy to recognize the actor by his devilish "Q" facial expressions, such as the cat that swallowed the canary grin, and that insidious laugh! Only one thing was missing. John was wearing a sedate (incognito?) wardrobe which included a silver tweed jacket, energetic pink shirt and dark slacks.

He immediately launched into a question and answer session, treating some questions seriously and having fun with those he couldn't, or wouldn't, answer, such as when someone asked when the fans would find out what happened to "Q" and Vash. "This is television, this is not a movie. You know what happened to Vash. I took her to another show and I drove her to suicide," he said happily. That was only part true, but he did take her to another show the following year—DEEP SPACE NINE.

One point he discussed was that year five was the only season of THE NEXT GENERATION which had no episode featuring Q. "I know there was an episode that seemed to be in the works and I was told about it. It was called 'Dueling Q's' or something like that. I expected that I was going to get called, but I never was. I was talking to Rick Berman (the producer of TNG) a couple days ago and he remarked that he'd been having trouble getting a really good 'Q' script. Hopefully this next one is, so I think it's better not to do a show that's bad than to try to go ahead and do it anyway. That's one of my theories about television. If they don't have anything on that's good, they should just have a blank screen. Then they should say to the actors, 'Do a good job next week and we aren't going to make you suffer through it [this week]. When I was at Gene's memorial, the producer/writer told me that he was working on an episode. And then I was told by Jonathan Frakes that I was shooting it, like in January, and then I think it just fell out. It certainly didn't get to the point where I ended up having a script in hand."

Referring to an episode where Q whispered in Data's ear and made him laugh, De Lancie was asked what he said to him. But he wouldn't tell. "I'll only tell if you do as good a job laughing as Brent did. That's our secret."

It has been established on THE NEXT GENERATION that Q and Guinan don't like each other, although the reason hasn't been specifically revealed. Asked what caused the enmity between them, De Lancie replied, "It was a bad date!"

THE LIFE OF An ACTOR

A fascinating point was raised regarding Q when De Lancie was asked if he enjoyed playing the villain? "I'm not the villain. I'm the hero. And yes, I enjoy it." And then there's that name. . why is he called Q? "You mean as opposed to 'S'? Or 'F'? You want the real answer? When I was in Scotland a woman came up to me and showed me a letter that Gene Roddenberry had

written to her saying that he was working on the new show, creating a new character in the pilot episode, and was going to name him after her. That just goes to prove—truth is more boring than fiction."

De Lancie had an interesting story about Roddenberry to tell about landing the role of Q. "I said before and I thought everybody knew—I slept with Gene Roddenberry," he said, laughing. "I auditioned just like everyone else. I will tell you a little story about my auditions. At the end of the second or third audition, he put his hand on my shoulder and said, 'You make my words sound even better than they are,' so I figured I had the job."

Since "Q" was initially just one character in one episode, De Lancie was asked whether he had any idea what playing that character would eventually accomplish for his career. "Well I'm omniscient so I knew everything," he remarked. "Gene Roddenberry came up to me about halfway through the show [the pilot episode] and we were just standing there and he said, 'You have no idea what you're getting yourself into!' And I have no idea what I've gotten myself into either. Who would think that this series would. . . even in the last couple of years it's kind of become mainstream. Now everybody knows about it. You don't even have to watch it. Now even people who don't watch STAR TREK know there's this whole subculture of weirdos and perverts."

On how his career began he said, "I started acting in high school, or maybe a little before that in 8th grade.

Our teacher came in and threw a book in my lap and said, 'You're going to do Henry IV' and I did HENRY IV at the end of the year. Then I kept on doing a lot of Shakespeare when I was in high school; we did about 6 or 7 plays. Then I went to college and I didn't want to be an actor. I don't know. Everybody wanted to me be an actor, so of course I decided that I wanted to be a political science major. It's one of those majors you pick if you don't know what you want to do. So I managed to live through the first 6 months of college not acting. And then I found myself doing a show. Then I ended up doing show after show after show. I went to Juilliard Performing Arts School in New York. Then at 26 years old I had my career crisis period when I realized that I didn't know how to do anything but acting. So I'd decided I'd better stick to acting and become more serious about it." But in spite of becoming a performer, he never cared to appear in a stage production for very long. "As an actor I can't stand to perform the same show for too long at a shot. About 6 weeks is my limit before I become bored. So I have chosen acting roles that don't require too much time away. However, I'm away enough that I can't participate in regular scheduled activities, either."

A CHILDHOOD STRUGGLE

Regarding what his motivation was to pursue acting, he said, "Well, I believe that acting was the most difficult thing I could do. It's still the most difficult thing I can do. You know I'm pretty good at organizing; I could run a company. There are a lot of things I could do. Acting kind of hits me where I've kept my greatest fear. I didn't know how to read for a very long time, and of course with acting you need to know how to read. I was not a very good student and yet with acting you need to have knowledge about many different things. Your research involves being a little bit of an art historian as well as a regular historian, and on and on and on. Also I think that psychologically it's interesting to me because ultimately the questions you ask of acting are the kind of fundamental questions of why and the exploration is a self-exploration. And those questions never change or never end. The answers are simply evolving. So that's the reason I got involved in acting."

John De Lancie's reference to his trouble with reading refers to his childhood problems with having dyslexia. But in spite of what all that had been like to deal with, he was willing to talk about it, possibly because he knew that others in the audience might well be experiencing similar problems.

"I guess my parents figured out I didn't know how to read when I was around 12 because I flunked out of school. Then I was tutored every day, 6 days a week until I was about 15. I went and auditioned for a show when I was 15 and we had to read it. I was a mess! I stammered and stuttered and simply couldn't read it. I made my way through it; sweat was dripping off me.

People were looking. It was awful. The next day I got a call saying that I got the part. I was so embarrassed by the experience the night before that I declined the part and then I realized that I needed to get this under control. So what I would do is read out loud. All my girlfriends in high school had to suffer through it. We would go out, but part of the deal was that I would read to them, and I read H.G. Wells, which is tough stuff. I don't know if you've read any H.G. Wells recently, but he clearly writes in the 19th century pattern. So I just continued to do that more and more and more. I just forced myself to read out loud."

But Dyslexia is not something which just goes away. It has to be confronted, dealt with, controlled and worked around. "I still have that problem. What I do to cover it is by making sure, first of all, that I get a script in time, and I can read it over easily. But when I begin to get nervous, the words on the page really get cloaked to me. It's never something I'm going to have great facility with. I have facility above and beyond what most of you have because that's my job. But I don't have the natural facility that some actors have who can quite literally read brilliantly the first time. So I guess the answer is, how did I overcome it? I found little things to do and worked at them a lot!"

THE DEMANDS
OF PERFORMING

De Lancie was enthusiastic in his praise of the cast of THE NEXT GENERATION, and of working with them he said, "It's swell, it's wonderful, and fab. It's a nice group of people and everybody works hard. I only work with them once per year. It used to be once per year. Now I think it's about 9. So I think the work that's involved in putting a television show together in a very short period of time really requires that most people behave themselves and work well and try to make things move along. And when I go to do the show I usually have a lot to do and don't have much time socializing and what have you. I do my job."

Although De Lancie was jocular and clearly having a good time with some of the questions, there were some subjects he dealt with seriously, such as when he was asked if he participated in organized sports. "My competition is mostly with myself," the actor explained, "and I don't enjoy taking games seriously. I feel that I need to have some place in my life that I don't take so seriously. For example, my sons are in soccer practice right now and you should see some of the fathers. These are little seven year olds! And the fathers are trying to kill each other.

"I also don't have a schedule that permits anything to be regulated. I can't say every Thursday I go to a practice game because my life just doesn't work that way. So I get up around 6:30 and go running. I work out with weights a little bit in my garage and that becomes my exercise program. I used to sail a lot and I still have a boat. People would say to me, 'Why don't you get into races?' That's not what I want. I want to be able to sail and then at 2:00 in the afternoon cocktail hour starts. I can just drink while I'm anchored. I feel I'm in a contending mode most of the time and I don't need to add to that."

IMAGINE HIM. . . NAKED

Asked whether he ever felt himself wanting to act like "Q" and play tricks on his neighbors, he said no. "I'm sure that my neighbors wouldn't appreciate my playing tricks on them either. It's funny, I feel like I've gone full circle. When I was in high school, my motto was to make today be funnier than yesterday and I spent up to age 26 finding everything was a big joke. But now it's not the same. I kind of put my humor in my work. I don't spend a lot of time doing it on the outside [on my personal time]. Maybe I should."

There was an episode in which "Q" appeared naked and he was asked whether he was actually wearing anything when he performed that scene? "That seems like a contradiction in terms—you were naked but were you wearing anything? No, I was naked. I was completely naked. So naked that I was completely naked. Actually when I first started out I had a jock strap on and it showed the lines. After all, you can't have something that tight and not have some sort of indent on your skin. So we're futzing around, trying to shoot it in a way that would be usable. Finally I said, 'To hell with it! People who want to stay, stay. People who want to go, go.

I'll take the jock strap off and let's shoot the damn thing.' So now I was completely naked."

In the same episode he was seen floating naked as well. "Well, that's actually kind of fun," De Lancie recalled. "Imagine being on a big sound stage with a blue screen behind me. The stage goes up as high as the length of this convention room goes. I've got a crew in front of me and a television monitor and they're shooting me standing straight up, okay? And I'm waving my arms sideways. What they've done is put the monitor on the side so that the image looks like I'm horizontal instead of vertical. So I'm waving my hands back and forth and waving everything but this," he said, pointing down to his groin area. "I'm good but I'm not that good. So that's how they did it. Then they take that image and superimpose it on another image of the crew and when they splice the two images together, the crew is turning towards me in the shot and somebody's head is in the way of the strategic position. There's a joke there," he says, cackling. "That's how it's done."

He was asked what his favorite episode is and whether he was naked in it? "Yes, it's in my contract that I'm to be naked in every episode. But they don't shoot that part. I just walk on and I'm naked. They amuse me in that way. Then they say, okay put your clothes on and let's start shooting.

"I don't have any really favorite episodes. I have snitches and snatches of things which I haven't looked at, frankly, since they were originally shot.

So some day I'll have to go through them and pick out some of those events."

FACETS OF ACTING

"You know," he continued, "a show is made up of so many different elements. And for myself, being one of the elements, my sense of it is much more critical. I don't look at it as a piece of entertainment. I look at it as some work. Don't misunderstand me, I'm very serious about my work."

But he's not trying to minimize the importance of working on the show when he says that it's just a job. "For me to say that STAR TREK is just a job is to make the differentiation that not having been a fan of the television show, but a fan of the movies, it is not like I walk on the set and I'm in awe. I come there to work. So to say it's just a job, it's not to minimize that factor. I take my job very seriously. I know your face, and when I do the show, metaphorically I know who I'm playing to. So I try to do as good a job as I possibly can. But I don't live the life of 'Q,' I work [on TNG] for one week out of the year."

De Lancie revealed some interesting behind-the-scenes information when he candidly discussed how the professional community as a whole views the realm of soap operas, since he once had a recurring role on DAYS OF OUR LIVES.

"It's a complicated thing to explain. DAYS OF OUR LIVES affords an actor the opportunity to act every day. It's also considered by the industry to be the sleaziest form of all. Soap opera actors have the least amount of respect. I had the best time on DAYS OF OUR LIVES. But I suffered in that people didn't take it seriously, and I didn't take it seriously. I miss the opportunity of performing and working every day, but I admire actors who can and need to perform every day, and their suffering from the lack of acknowledgment that the rest of the industry gives them. So I find myself kind of downplaying what I do because I know there's a part of them than envies what I do. Acting is a very difficult profession to do and perform, and it's too bad that there's such a strong and prejudicial attitude about one kind of acting as opposed to another. Many actors in this country identify their careers by what they don't do. For instance, 'I don't do commercials, but I do pilots, but I don't do episodics, but I do movies,' and on and on and on. In the end many of them don't do anything. In the end you have to walk this thin line."

LIFE ON THE FRONT LINE

Asked whether there's things he hasn't done that he really wanted to do, De Lancie explained, "Yes, all the time. Work comes to us from the future, not from the past when you're a commercial actor. So if I said, 'I'd like to work with Peter Weir,' you can say it. You can dream it, maybe. But it's just not part of the usual thinking that goes on. As far as working with Peter Weir, of course I'd say, 'Oh, yes!' Any of the great film makers; of course I'd like to work with them. But I haven't defined a list of people that I'd need to work with because that's so much out of my control that it would be maybe just wasted time."

Since some of the regular actors on THE NEXT GENERATION have done some directing, De Lancie was asked whether he had aspirations along those lines. "Well, I've directed a lot of things in the theater, but I've never directed anything on film. I'm going back tomorrow to set up something that a bunch of my students are doing right now and I'm directing those pieces. I've enjoyed directing quite a bit and I'm going to probably move toward that pretty soon in a more sustained way. But my acting career seems to be progressing every year, so I don't want to let that go as well. I'm not terribly interested in jumping into the fray of directing television. It is a producer's medium and directors aren't handled any better than actors are. So I just don't.

"Ultimately it's always the material in the end. If you're dealing with material that, for the most part, is just crap, I don't know why I would jump from being an actor that works with crap to a director that works with crap. It doesn't have all that much allure. In theater you're usually dealing with very 'past' material, and in that respect, the best of the past material. Most of the time it's a lot more fun—a lot more challenging."

Does he want to be a writer? "Sounds like everyone wants me to do something other than what I'm doing. I don't want to be a writer, though. That's the other thing that writers have, is that writers write scripts and they're all thrown out. They're changed immediately. There's a saying in our business, that what the writer does is they present their scripts to the producers and then they all sit around and piss on it for awhile."

THE POWER BROKERS IN TELEVISION

De Lancie explained that the problem with the entertainment business is that few of those on the creative and performing end have any sort of control over their own work and how it's used. "The writers are out of control, unless you get into the top four. As a director you're out of control; as an actor you're out of control. After all, you may do 3 or 4, or 24 takes of a scene. But you're not the one who picks the take that's best. There are many different people looking at the takes and they might choose the one in which the flower in the background is focused. You know, your performance might be great in the one before that. So I'm not anxious to jump into other careers that have little control. I write a good deal, but it's mostly letters. I'm kind of a Boswell, and where they're going they don't get edited."

So who has control in television? "There are people in the business who have control but they have to be the top directors, and even they will have long discussions about how they've had to compromise their way to get there, or they've found themselves in a compromising position. It's very few people who get to do what they really want. There are just too many people involved. If you can finance your own film, great. But most people can't and so that's not how it works.

"But sometimes the compromise is good," he added. "Sometimes you get to work with a great bunch of people. For the most part I have this 10% rule. 10% of anything is good and the rest of it is not so good. So 10% of the movies are good, 10% of plays are good, 10% of scripts are good, and 10% of books seems to be a fair number. One out of 10 books really grab you, the rest kind of go on."

BRINGING A CHARACTER TO LIFE

Asked whether he ever finds himself overextended with not enough free time, De Lancie stated, "No, most actors want to work all the time and I don't find myself over-extended. I wish I were working more, and I think that time will come. And you see, the other thing is that I work as a freelancer which is very different than being on the show. I'm a driftal character on the show, but in 5 episodes I've been able to make an impact. I was a driftal character on DAYS OF OUR LIVES but I had the least amount of air time, so that made an impact. I don't like to work full time, and I don't look forward to being on a long running television show. There's something grueling about that. I'm much better off when I'm a little antsy

and things change within a two to three month period. My wife is terrific at doing long runs on stage shows. She could be on a show 5-6 months a year. I'm just dying on a show after 6 weeks."

How can an actor make an impact in just five episodes? Is it the ability to steal scenes, to get attention or is it just a natural part of his personality? De Lancie revealed one of his secrets and it involves intelligence. "To steal scenes!" he laughs. "I seem to get those characters, or at least I seem to prevail or perceive the opportunity where that can take place. What I did with DAYS OF OUR LIVES was very organized. I was hired to come in and play a psychopath for 5 days. I took a look at the show the day before and I said they want a psychopath, they need a comedian. I will turn this psychopath into a comedian. I'll still kill, but I'll laugh. I also made a determination that soap opera characters seem to be socially polite but personally dysfunctional. Therefore I chose to be socially impolite but personally functional. And try as they would to make me the village idiot, the audience began to see me as the truth teller. That's just knowing your craft.

"In HAND THAT ROCKS THE CRADLE they brought me in to audition for the lead. I said to the director, you need me to play the lead, but you won't hire me to play the lead. Now that's the truth. So I want to play the gynie [gynecologist]. He said why? Because if it's played well, it will be remembered. It will be the part that's remembered, and you need that part to be played well enough so that through the whole movie that has a residual effect. Now in the end, I think that they needed me to play the lead. Just because I feel that it was one of those instances where, in a horror film, it's important that you do not lose the credibility of what the character is doing.

"Ultimately the film was supposed to be about 2 women and that's what it was about and not necessarily anything more. But I thought that the husband was played in such a way that you began to just not believe him after awhile. So I chose to try out for the other role in the hopes that they would accept me for that, and they did. So in a way I kind of gravitate towards that."

THE CRAFT OF ACTING

Although it might be interesting if John De Lancie were reteamed with the woman who played his wife on DAYS OF OUR LIVES, the actor doubts such a thing would happen for very good reasons.

"First of all this is a truth in our business—nobody watches anything. The producers, directors, writers or actors have no idea who's working on anything else. This is a blanket statement that's not completely correct. But it's the general gist of the way in which the industry works. So as popular as we were, it did not transcend to the point of where [Rick] Berman would say, 'Oh my God. What a fabulous idea to have John and Arlene together.' Now Arlene and I did another show recently called DIRTY LAUNDRY, which you won't see. But it was a pilot for CBS. Arlene wrote it and it was a marvelous pilot. There were 3 couples in

the show and it was a very sexy, psychologically astute show/comedy with Fran Tresher, Mark Singer, myself and Arlene. That was an attempt to get us back together again, but it didn't work. I mean, it was her show but understand, nobody cast me to get Arlene and I back together again. I had to go in and audition just like everyone else."

John De Lancie has a certain preference as to the kind of roles he likes to play. "My preference is to play characters that will be open to the line. When he begins with the show, you are not quite sure where the character is going to end. See, most actors play characters that you can pretty well plot. During the first 5 or 6 minutes of the show you can say, oh, they're going to end up here or there. I don't like to play characters that way. I like to make sure that if I play some sort of evil character that I play it as though he were your brother. Some characters that are villains are played so that you know they are villains. But in real life, when you hear about the Jeffrey Dahmers of the world, what you always hear is the neighbors saying, 'We had no idea! He's such a quiet and well behaved. . . little monster.' And I don't think in the world of drama, that's always considered like, 'Oh, isn't that clever to play him so opposite of being evil.' But in real life, that's the way it is.

"In any case, I do that. I try to make sure we've got a bunch of flip flops because I think it's fun for you. It's certainly more fun for me. There's nothing more boring than being an actor of a character that's the same all the way through. I try my damnedest and sometimes I'm successful. Many times the directors don't feel that way. They want the character played straight, like when the script says, 'Oh, I'm really happy to see you.' But wouldn't it be nice to say it like a part of it sounded like you weren't happy? It always opens it up and it makes for different interpretations. That's what's called character acting. That's not what the melodramas were. They were caricatures; they were two dimensional characters. We're much more into an acting that is psychological now. So I just find it interesting that there would be a number of different levels of interpretation. One person will say, 'Well, he really is happy to see you!' The other person says, 'No, I don't think so. I think there's something underneath all that,' and that's what I try to do."

CHAPTER 6

Daniel Davis says that he and Patrick Stewart were both trained in theatre.
Here Patrick Stewart attends the 13th Annual Ace Awards at the Pantages Theatre in Hollywood on Jan. 12, 1992.

Whoopi Goldberg is also a very theatrical actress.
Here she appears decked out in her finest at the 65th Annual Academy Awards on March 29, 1993.

Season six of THE NEXT GENERATION saw Daniel Davis reprise
his role of Professor Moriarty in the sequel to the second season episode "Elementary, Dear Data." On March 7,
1993, the actor appeared as a guest at the VULKON convention.

CHAPTER 6
DANIEL DAVIS: PROFESSOR MORIARTY

By Diana Collins

To introduce Daniel Davis more completely to the audience here, a video was shown featuring highlights of his movie and television roles. Then the actor gallantly sauntered toward center stage amid enthusiastic applause. Daniel sported a distinctly non-Victorian looking black sports jacket, white shirt and nicely fitted denim jeans. Yet who could mistake those flashing steel blue eyes, aristocratic beige curled coif with gray temples, and mischievously calculating grin for anyone but our favorite misunderstood arch-villain, Professor Moriarty?

Daniel Davis looked out toward the crowd with a very pleasantly shocked expression for the warm reception at this, his first convention. Davis stated that he was very curious about the audience and what we wanted to know about him. Thus he asked if it would be best to begin by fielding questions? The first question dealt with the comedy sequences in his introductory video and what they were from.

"Those clips were from a show called FRANK'S PLACE," Davis explained. "It was only on the air for one season and it was directed and written by a brilliant man named Hugh Wilson, who also did a show called WKRP. He's a very talented man. That particular episode was one of the most fun episodes that I think he did on the series. It's because Hugh was sort of paying back some of the people that he had to work with in the industry. There were a lot of in-jokes throughout the entire script.

"Comedy is something I love to do," the actor added. "In fact, this past week I've just signed to do a pilot for a new comedy series for the Fall. It's called THE NANNY. We will start production the third week of March. Then we find out in mid-June whether CBS is interested in taking it to series. So we will be on pins and needles until summer. But it's a very funny comedy. I play a sort of quintessential stuffy English father and it's a very funny part."

THE NEMESIS IS IN

Davis was complimented for portraying a very different and much more interesting version of Moriarty on THE NEXT GENERATION and asked what direction the character might go in the future?

"Thank you for paying such a nice compliment about the work. I have played a lot of characters like Moriarty in the theater. For me, those people are never villains in their own lives. They're only villains in someone else's life. In their own life they're the hero and they have very strong desires, very strong goals, and very strong objectives. The world has twisted their mind or twisted their behavior or something. I always look for the psychology of their character; the kind that led them off in the wrong direction. But I still think of them basically as good people who do bad things, if that makes sense. They're not bad people doing bad things."

The actor pointed out that the world is full of television writing which

portrays only the opposite extremes of good and evil, black and white. "What's really interesting for all of us are the gray areas, and that's why I like to work with a character like Moriarty that's many shades of gray. Because if it's all black or all white, it's a little tedious for the actor and the audience. To make a human being out of Moriarty is my goal.

"Each time that I've played Moriarty, I realized that the writers and producers want to take the character away from the Moriarty that we know from Sherlock Holmes and those stories whose arch villain has been left behind. They're taking him in a direction that has to do with consciousness and being, what it is and what it means to be a human being. What defines a human being and makes him distinct from the animal world. And also in this case, if a fictional character realizes that he is a fictional character, as Moriarty has, and wants to become a human being—that's a very interesting direction. So I hope the writers and producers will be pursuing that."

WORKING ON THE ENTERPRISE

When asked what it was like to work with Patrick Stewart, and whether they had any plans to work together again, Davis replied, "Patrick and I both have theater background. He worked many roles in England before he came to this role. I worked in regional theater in the United States for about 20 years before I really got interested in working in front of the camera. So he and I have very similar ways of working. Our processes are very similar. We speak the same sort of actor language. We work very well together and like each other very much. He's one of the easiest people to be around and one of the most professional."

Some fans would like to see Daniel Davis and Patrick Stewart working together again, outside of STAR TREK. In explaining the logistical problems involved with accomplishing a project like that, Davis explained, "We work many long hours; 14-16 hours per day sometimes. Very long hours on STAR TREK. They're the hardest working actors in Hollywood, I think. Patrick had done a play in England a few years ago. But with schedules in Los Angeles and England, trying to get everybody free at the same time was just too difficult. A TV show takes 7 days. A play takes 6-8 weeks to rehearse. Then you have to guarantee a run of two or three months for the producers to be able to make some money back on their investment. So it's very hard to get three or four months out of the life of a busy actor like Patrick, and hopefully, like me."

An interesting point was raised when Davis was asked why none of the actors on THE NEXT GENERATION have ever received an Emmy Award for their performances?

"The answer has something to do with the fact that the show is syndicated and doesn't have a network behind it because it's in different markets around the country. That's a big part of the success of a show and how it gets nominated. Many of the people who are nominated or vote also work for various networks, so they look out for their own. I think that probably has more to do with it

than anything."

LIFE ON STAGE AND IN SPACE?

Since Daniel Davis has extensive theatrical experience, he was asked about this and whether the audiences are different between the east coast and the west coast?

"I've played in theaters all over the country and in Canada," the actor stated. "I've spent a lot of years touring in plays and in various regional theaters throughout the country. I've found that there are differences in audiences. But the differences are subtle. Sometimes we find surprising reactions in audiences in places that you didn't expect. You think that you're in a very sophisticated city and you're going to have a very sophisticated crowd. But you'll have a crowd that doesn't respond at all.

"That symbiotic relationship between the audience and the actor is one of the most curious and exciting relationships that you can experience, because you are responsible for how we do, in a certain way," he said referring to how an audience can affect a live performance. "I mean, we prepare, bring you something, and then your response is either egging us on or aspersing us. So it's a very tied relationship, which is something that, working in film and television, you really miss. I know you hear actors say all the time that live theater experience is preferable because of the audience's response, but it really is exciting to be able to hear. It's one of the reasons why I love coming to this convention because I had no idea what [television] audiences thought about Moriarty!"

The subject of NASA came up and he was asked what he thought of the state of the space program in light of how much STAR TREK makes people want to explore those brave new worlds out there?

"I hope that one of the things that Mr. Clinton will do is take some of the defense jobs that were being lost because of peace time and have them turned over to NASA. I'd love to see that happen because I'd love to see us go there. I want to go there myself. So I definitely want to see that happen."

A CLASSICAL ACTOR FROM ARKANSAS

In spite of the fact that Davis has an accent that sounds British, he revealed that actually he's from Arkansas.

"When people would ask where are you from? It used to be that people from Arkansas would say, I'm from Ar. . . mumble, mumble and let it go by. And then President Clinton changed all that. Now I can say, 'Hi, I'm from Arkansas.' Now in four more years I'll be saying, 'Hi, I'm from Ar. . . mumble, mumble,' again. I hope not.

"I'm a classical actor. I don't know why or where I got that idea because I didn't even see a classical play before I did one. So I don't know where I got the idea of being a classical actor. As part of my classical training I quickly lost my Arkansas accent and developed a mid-Atlantic accent. It almost sounds British,

but it's not.

"I grew up in a very small town in Arkansas that had 2,000 people in it. My mother and father were born and raised in this town. They met each other in grade school and they were married in high school and they never dated anybody but each other. My father ran the motion picture theater, among other things. I should write a short story about this some day because there was a place called 'the crying room.' It was a room which was sealed off in the movie theater. It was soundproof. It had a sort of camera box where people with infants could sit in there with their babies and watch the movie and not be disturbing other patrons. My father ran the projection and my mother sold the tickets and the concession. I was put in my high chair in the crying room and I watched movies from the time I was a year and a half on. That, I think, more than anything is why I wanted to be an actor.

"As I got to be an adult, I started trying to work out my psychology, about my childhood; about my youth and the things that affected me. I would go to my parents and say, 'Remember when such and such happened?' And they'd say, 'No, that never happened.' Then about 6 years ago I was sitting up one night watching the American Movie Classics and some of the old really bad B movies came on. And I thought, that's what I was talking about. When I asked my parents when such and such happened, it was the plot of this movie. So now I'm spending the rest of my adult life trying to figure out if my memories are mine or if they're from movies."

THE LIFE OF AN ACTOR

Asked whether he watched THE NEXT GENERATION before he appeared on the show, Davis stated that he had not. "I had watched STAR TREK back in the '60s when I was in high school and became a fan right away. I was totally flabbergasted when I first walked on the set. It was just the most exciting thing that I'd ever possibly experienced! The absolute reality, you know? It didn't seem like a set at all. You can walk around. They have two sound stages, as I'm sure you know, that are dedicated to the Enterprise itself. Then there's a third sound stage for which they build the special sets for each episode, and it is absolutely real! You have no sense of being on a set.

"I have a friend who's a devoted fan. When I told him I was doing an episode, that was his first impression after being on the set with me, that he became 10 years old again. So he went home and bought a space suit for the show. He was inspired, but he was just very touched that it all happened."

Davis had an interesting response when asked when he was able to quit his regular job to be an actor.

"I never had one. I mean, I was an actor from the time I was a child. I started out on a local television program in Arkansas when I was seven years old. It was on every day after school. I was on that show until I was about 13. Then from that I went to working in community theater and in college theater. Then I trained at a conservatory to go on to be professional. When I got to New York and started my career, I wasn't quite greeted with the open arms the way I thought it would be. Here I was in New York thinking I'd take the town by storm. And of course no one's waiting for you. So I had to do a lot of things to keep life and limb together. I've done nearly every kind of job. The one thing I haven't done is the actor's job, which is wait tables. It's the only thing I didn't do. I sold shoes, worked as a file clerk, and did everything else. But I was not a waiter. I guess when I left New York in 1974, which I had arrived at in 1968, I went to San Francisco to join the American Conservatory Theater, which is a company. I stayed there for 7 years. I've never stopped working as an actor or an entertainer in a job ever since 1974."

THE RETURN OF MORIARITY?

On the subject of special effects and what it's like to work with them, Davis explained, "It usually adds one full day of work to your schedule for one thing because they take such an enormous time to do. They are very intricate and very tricky and in order to do, for instance, the Transporter room, or an appearance or a disappearance, you have to be absolutely stark still for a certain amount of time on the camera. Then when you reappear, you have to make sure you are in the exact same physical relationship that you were before. And sometimes it's 2 or 3 days between shooting the disappearance and shooting the reappearance. So it's just hard keeping it all in your head. Fortunately the supervisor watches every move and reminds you of every single thing you did and the way you did it. It was time consuming.

"Stephanie Gräff and I were sitting in the shuttle craft, at the end of the second episode, "Moriarty." They were shooting us going off into space. We were looking at a blue screen. We had asked the special effects people to come over and describe to us what we were actually seeing. We had no idea. They came over to the set and said, 'We haven't decided yet.' " Davis laughed at the memory of this. "We don't know what we're going to be seeing. We think it's going to be some kind of nova, but we're not exactly sure. So they said, 'Just be really happy and wide-eyed to see it.' So you have to make it all up in your head. You just have to use your imagination. So I imagine Stephanie was thinking about one thing, and I was thinking about something else. Maybe I was thinking about Stephanie," he said, chuckling. "So I've no idea what it's like until I'm seeing the finished product. I'm seeing it for the first time when you're seeing it, and it's always as exciting for me as it is for you all to see."

He was asked the inevitable question about whether a future episode was planned in which Moriarty would realize that he is still a part of the holodeck.

"I just don't know. I said yesterday that he's sitting in that little cube on Captain Picard's coffee table. And if somebody knocks it off or steps on it, my life is over. But I think that there are so many ways that this could go. I think that the cube is probably the least problem that the writers will face. It's just that. . . we're out of the cube; what happened to the cube? The same thing that happened to that piece of paper I drew on in the first episode. We don't talk about it any more. We just go on. I don't know where or even if they're going to be able to find a way or a place to take it. I've had a lot of reaction from the fans and they do seem to want it back, so write and let the producers and writers know. I do have a real fantasy notion of at least one storyline that I would like to do. I don't know how and I don't write the stories. But I would love to see Moriarty and 'Q' face one another. Talk about ego? I don't know if the universe is big enough to contain the two of them."

ACTING ON TV AND THE STAGE

Regarding acting techniques and whether there are different approaches used for television, film or the stage, the actor stated, "Yes. There was a conflict until I learned the difference because I'd come into television by way of a daytime soap opera in New York. I hadn't worked on television since my childhood days. Then I came to New York and was doing a play called 'Amadeus' and I was doing a soap opera called TEXAS in the daytime. I suddenly found that, especially soap operas, can view just the eyes some

NEXT GENERATION

time. And that was very frightening to see, if you had a 31 inch screen, to see 31 inches of eyes. I realized that all I had to do was to just think, and I was emoting. Most of my body was probably out of shot of the camera, so that I might keep everything very contained. Then in Los Angeles, I moved to working on a single camera to close the show, done on film, as opposed to tape which is done with three or four cameras at the same time getting all the angles set.

With a single camera, they reset for every angle. I learned very quickly, I don't even think in terms of size any more except to bring it down and make it as concentrated, as focused and as intense as you can with eye communication. I was always going in to find another actor, and just lock eyes. That's the way it worked."

Asked about the differences between Moriarty and other roles he's done, Davis explained, "My process for working as an actor is pretty much the same no matter what cut or what week I find myself in, whether it's a play, or television show, film, whatever. You really start with the script; you start with the words. You start with what you have to say and what is said about you; what is said about your character by other people. I'm going to talk a little technical actor jargon here—you pick up an objective of each scene. What is the reason for coming in the room and why do I stay there? What do I need? What do I want? What do I have to have before I can leave this room? You decide what that objective is, pick out what are the obstacles to you to getting that objective. That is part of the vocabulary of the actors working on it

from that standpoint.

"As an actor you are given the circumstances of a scene, or a character like Moriarty, who is fictional, but based on an idea, novel, short story or whatever. That Moriarty finds himself in deep space, in another century. And this is a very strong 19th century mind. He suddenly finds himself in the 24th century, with technology that he doesn't understand. Yet everything the computer knows, Moriarty knows, because he's been programmed to be smarter than Data. So he has a lot of knowledge that he doesn't have a practical application for. He's a very complicated mind. His eyes and his mind, everything is going all the time. He's like a sponge, just absorbing everything and everyone around him. He realizes very early in the first episode that he is not a villain. Remember the line Moriarty says, 'Whatever I was when this began, I have grown.' That is truthfully how he feels. He has made a very quick evolution from a fictional to a real person in his own mind. Just to become corporeal and leave the holodeck and to live. That is what he strives for, that is if I ever come back as Moriarty again."

LIFE AFTER MORIARTY

How did he land that plum role in those two episodes of THE NEXT GENERATION?

"The casting director on the show is Junie Lowry-Johnson. She has been wonderful over the years about exploring the theater, going to regional theaters around the country and finding actors who do classical work. The scripts on

69

STAR TREK are so literal, so full of technical jargon that it is difficult to perform. In some ways the technical science words are comparable to learning Shakespeare's English. And STAR TREK is a tightly constructed five act play. So the rigor of classical training helped me to prepare for this kind of work."

Asked who his favorite person to work with on THE NEXT GENERATION was, Davis answered, "My favorite person would probably have to be Patrick because I've had the most to do with him. Also, for the reasons I've said earlier, that we just talk the same language. We have kind of a rapport, a chemistry between us, and we really don't have to talk about it very much. We find that we don't rehearse very much. We just sort of figure out where we're going to stand, and where the camera wants us to be, and then we just start. We just sort of do it. It has a real power in the take, so I've enjoyed Patrick the most. I've enjoyed working with Brent and LeVar; they're really the only people I worked with on the show. And Stephanie, the last time, and she was a guest, not one of the regular people."

Daniel Davis had some interesting observations on how his personal and professional life has changed due to his high profile role as Prof. Moriarty on those two episodes of THE NEXT GENERATION.

"Well, I had no idea until this weekend that there was any recognizability at all. I'm just stunned, except I did get a hint of it last spring. I went to Paris and I was walking along the Champs-Elysees and a young teenage couple came up to me and said," in a perfectly smooth French accent," Moriarty! I said yes and proceeded to walk on as I thought, 'My God! Recognized in Paris? I have surely arrived!'

"I've enjoyed being able to work as an actor in television, film, and mostly on the stage. I've enjoyed the fact that I've kept a certain amount of anonymity about me because I think it's dangerous for actors to expose too much of themselves to the public because it begins to diminish your power as an actor. It's more interesting sometimes for the work to speak for you. In some ways I feel that my work is the most interesting thing about me and one of the most interesting things for you to know about me. I feel that other things might cloud your appreciation of my work and I wouldn't want that to get in the way. Sometimes I fear because television has such enormous power to expose you and your identity. I think the country is in this sort of grip of mania for self-exposure. And the talk shows—if I hear Rosanne Barr talk about her childhood one more time, I think I will go mad. I don't think that's what we should do. I think that other than STAR TREK, and if this new series NANNY goes well in the Fall, my life won't change much."

CHAPTER 7

The classic Vulcan of them all is Leonard Nimoy's Spock.
Here Nimoy appears at the Star Trek press conference at Paramount Studio on Mar. 28, 1978.

Patrick Stewart's Captain Picard formed a mind link with the Vulcan Sarek.
Here Stewart appears at the tribute held for the Next Generation on March 14, 1992 in Los Anfeles.

Photo credit: Albert Ortega, ©1993 Ron Galella Ltd.

As vital as Vulcans have been to the original STAR TREK series and its subsequent motion pictures, it is surprising how neglected this ancient race has been on THE NEXT GENERATION. Only three episodes have featured Vulcans prominently, and these also served to unite old the STAR TREK with the new.

CHAPTER 7
THE VULCAN TRILOGY
By M. P. Sakai

In the original STAR TREK series, no alien race caught the public's fancy quite as much as the Vulcans, or "Vulcanians," as they were even referred to in one memorable mistake in an early episode. And no wonder. As portrayed by Leonard Nimoy, James T. Kirk's science officer Spock was a fascinating blend of basic human emotions and cool alien aloofness. Audiences envied his remarkable self control, yet secretly yearned to see his vulnerable side exposed. The writers of the original series were not ones to pass up such inherent dramatic possibilities, and came up with a number of scenarios in which the Vulcan's exterior veneer cracked in a variety of ways.

Public reaction to the Spock character was so overwhelming that the first episode of STAR TREK's second season, "Amok Time" written by Theodore Sturgeon, took its viewers to Spock's mysterious home world of Vulcan, revealing shocking secrets about the mating practices of Spock's people Even though the budgetary limitations of the original series allowed for a very simplified presentation of the planet Vulcan, it was depicted in broad, effective strokes. This was aided immeasurably by the casting of Celia Lovsky (Peter Lorre's one-time wife) as the eminent Vulcan T'Pau, who carried the entire weight of an implied culture in her bearing.

Later that season, more was revealed about Spock in D.C. Fontana's script for "Journey To Babel," which introduced Spock's father Sarek and his human mother Amanda, and explored the troubled relationship between father and son against the backdrop of a murder mystery.

Plenty happened to Spock in the decades after those memorable episodes. Having his brain stolen didn't slow him down; neither did death and transfiguration in the STAR TREK movies many years later. Other Vulcans also appeared in supporting roles in the STAR TREK movies, including several key appearances by Sarek, portrayed on film, as in the series, by veteran actor Mark Lenard.

THE ELUSIVE VULCANS

When STAR TREK: THE NEXT GENERATION made its television debut in 1988, it was notable for its lack of any Vulcan characters. It was the intent of the new program to focus on new alien races. The premiere episode, "Encounter At Farpoint," did have a link with the STAR TREK of the 1960s in the form of a cameo appearance by DeForest Kelley as Dr. Leonard McCoy. More than a few people wondered whether or not it would have made more sense to use Spock, with his extended Vulcan life span, as the old guard's official "seal of approval" on the newly launched series.

Vulcans were few and far between in THE NEXT GENERATION. They were sometimes referred to, or perhaps glimpsed in the background, but no Vulcan character ever appeared on THE NEXT GENERATION until the second season episode "The Schizoid Man." This featured a one-shot Vulcan

character, the female Dr. Selar. Even in this instance, the Vulcan character was incidental to the story line. Her place could easily have been filled by Dr. Crusher or (considering that this was the second season) Dr. Pulaski.

The third season episode "Who Watches The Watchers" featured a race known as the Mentakans, who looked like Vulcans and apparently had a culture similar to early Vulcan society, but this was as far as that went.

The Vulcan shortage was finally remedied with the third season episode "Sarek," which starred Mark Lenard in the title role. THE NEXT GENERATION had always taken place in the same history as the STAR TREK movies and the original series, but this was the first time that a major character crossover had taken place. (McCoy's cameo appearance in "Encounter At Farpoint" was barely acknowledged as the character was never identified by name in the story. DeForest Kelley might just as well have been playing another character entirely!)

The continuity of the entire series was strengthened with the appearance of Sarek. The episode included such revelations as the fact that, as a young officer, Jean-Luc Picard had attended Spock's wedding. This was the first time that Spock had even been referred to on THE NEXT GENERATION, and it was obvious from these references that everyone's favorite Vulcan was definitely still alive. After all, he was a good deal younger that his father's two-hundred plus years. Immediately, a guest shot by Leonard Nimoy became a much hoped-for possibility for countless viewers of STAR TREK: THE NEXT GENERATION.

VULCAN SURPRISES

The fourth season of THE NEXT GENERATION saw no such crossover with Mr. Spock. The episode "Data's Day" did feature a Vulcan ambassador named T'Pel, but she turned out to be a Romulan spy posing as a Vulcan.

And so THE NEXT GENERATION carried on without any further significant representation of Vulcans, until it was announced, right before the beginning of the fifth season, that the quintessential Vulcan would finally be appearing on the show: Leonard Nimoy had signed to reprise the role of Spock in a two-part episode! This would finally establish an even stronger link between the two best-documented periods of TREK history, and would do so in no uncertain terms. The events of the episodes entitled "Unification" would be inspired by Spock's memories of the events in the then-forthcoming STAR TREK VI: THE UNDISCOVERED COUNTRY, which would, in turn examine the first steps toward the peace settlement between the Federation and the Klingon Empire. This would even include an appearance by Michael Dorn as a direct ancestor of his NEXT GENERATION character, Worf.

While THE NEXT GENERATION has not featured a great many stories involving Vulcans,

three of its episodes— "Sarek" and the two parts of "Unification"— have been very important stories about that intriguing species. These three episodes are worthy of closer examination.

THE SECRET OF THE AMBASSADOR

The breakthrough third season episode "Sarek" was directed by Les Landau from a teleplay by renowned fantasist Peter S. Beagle, author of such novels as A FINE AND PRIVATE PLACE and THE LAST UNICORN. Beagle's script for "Sarek" was developed from an original story by Marc Cushman and Jake Jacobs.

The episode opens as the Federation is about to enter negotiations with an elusive alien race, the Legarans. The Enterprise, as the flagship of Starfleet, has been chosen to host this important meeting, and the Federation's emissary is none other than the 202-year old Vulcan Ambassador, Sarek. Picard is pleased to welcome such a distinguished personage aboard.

The Ambassador's arrival is preceded by two assistants; one human, and the other a younger Vulcan named Sakkath. The aides insist that Ambassador Sarek must rest upon his arrival and isn't up to receiving visitors. Picard is sorry that the Ambassador cannot attend any social functions, but he invites Perrin, Sarek's second wife, (a human like his first wife Amanda) to a recital of

Mozart compositions that evening. To everyone's surprise, the elusive Sarek joins his wife at the recital. Picard, seated behind the Ambassador, observes a tear run down Sarek's face, as if the music had affected him emotionally. Sarek rises and departs in a hurry moments after this occurs, leaving Picard rather perplexed.

Strange tensions begin to develop among the crew of the Enterprise, culminating in a huge brawl in Ten Forward. Even Commander Riker is hit in the ensuing melee. Deanna Troi reveals to Picard that she had sensed that the Vulcan ambassador experienced a loss of emotional control at the recital. Dr. Crusher puts forward the possibility that this might be a symptom of Ben Dai Syndrome, a disease which affects Vulcans of advanced age. If this is what is causing Sarek to lose control of his emotions, then his Vulcan telepathy may be the cause of the strange disruptions among the crew, broadcasting, in effect, his emotional disturbances to everyone around him.

A FINAL CONQUEST

When confronted with this possibility, Sarek's human assistant will admit to nothing. But when pressed, the Vulcan aide, Sakkath, cannot lie, and tells Data that he has been using his own telepathic abilities to help Sarek maintain emotional control.

All this has been done without Sarek's knowledge or approval, and he dismisses Sakkath when he discovers what he has been doing. He denies

that he has Ben Dai Syndrome, but reluctantly agrees to undergo a test for the disease. However, Sarek refuses to postpone the negotiation until the results are in. Picard tries to force the issue: if Sarek is ill, it will almost certainly have a serious negative effect on the negotiations. Sarek becomes furious and loses control entirely. Once he calms down, he cannot help but admit to himself, and to Picard, that he is ill.

There is, however, a means of proceeding with the negotiations. It involves a mind meld between the Captain and the Ambassador. This will be a trade-off of sorts in which Sarek will be able to use Picard's self-control while Picard acts as a repository for Sarek's turbulent emotions. With this accomplished, Sarek goes on to complete the negotiations, which are a total success. But while that is taking place, Picard must contend with Sarek's long unvoiced emotions, including his sense of loss regarding the death of his first wife, Amanda, and his love for his son Spock, long buried beneath the disappointment and anger he has always felt at his son's chosen way of life.

Picard endures this difficult period, and as a result manages to learn more about the Vulcan ambassador than he had ever dreamed possible. Sarek reverses the mind meld before it can injure Picard, and the Ambassador, realizing that he has passed the stage where he can continue in his duties, retires to Vulcan with his wife, his lengthy career capped by one more remarkable diplomatic success.

"Sarek" was a truly dramatic episode, with a superb guest appearance by Mark Lenard as the faltering ambassador. Patrick Stewart was no slouch here either, as his scene alone in Sarek's quarters after the mind meld was easily one of his best pieces of acting. The references to Spock were more than off-hand references to the old show. They were a crucial part of this character study of Sarek, who emerges here as more than just a character who pops up from time to time to check up on Spock.

Sarek becomes a deep, complex, and well-rounded character through the unusual technique of having another character take charge of his emotions. No other series could possibly have pulled that stunt off—but on STAR TREK: THE NEXT GENERATION, it worked like a charm.

THE MYSTERIOUS MR. SPOCK

Spock's much-heralded appearance on THE NEXT GENERATION occurred at the end of the fifth season episode "Unification I." While Spock was not actually seen in person until the very last scene, he was present very much in spirit throughout the story. "Unification I" was directed by Les Landau from a teleplay by Jeri Taylor (from a story by Rick Berman and Michael Piller). Sarek is also a major player in the drama.

"Unification" begins on Stardate 45233.1. The Enterprise has been recalled to a nearby starbase. Captain Picard is ushered in to a private meeting with Fleet Admiral Brackett. The subject of their meeting is a touchy one: a leading Federation ambassador disappeared three weeks earlier, only to resurface on the planet Romulus. It is feared that this ambassador may have defected. The Admiral has obtained a single intelligence image of the ambassador on Romulus, and shows it to Picard. It reveals that the ambassador in question is a person who Picard recognizes immediately: Spock. Picard's assignment is to discover why Spock left Federation space so abruptly, and what he is doing on Romulus.

The Enterprise journeys to the planet Vulcan, where Picard plans to visit Sarek. After all, they became rather intimately acquainted the last time they met, and Picard is hoping that Sarek can shed some light on the motives behind his son's apparent actions. En route, the Enterprise salvages a crashed Ferengi ship from an asteroid belt. There are traces of Vulcan metal in this wreck, but Geordi is unable to determine the significance.

When Picard beams down to Vulcan, he discovers that Sarek is gravely ill. Perrin is at first unwilling to let Captain Picard see Sarek. She informs the Captain that Spock did not visit his father before his mysterious departure, and therefore she cannot imagine what light Sarek could possibly shed on Spock's actions. But she relents out of consideration for the great assistance that Picard rendered her husband during their previous encounter.

SAREK'S LAST WORDS

Sarek is, quite literally, on his deathbed, and his emotions frequently overpower him as death draws ever nearer. He does not even recognize Picard until Jean-Luc tells him that Spock is missing. Sarek is shocked to discover that his son has gone to Romulus, although he knew that Spock had made the acquaintance of a Romulan senator named Pardek.

Spock had long maintained the controversial position that an open dialogue with the Romulans is an important goal for the Federation, but the notion that Spock would defect to the Romulans is utterly implausible. Spock must have some other reason for going to Romulus. Sarek begins to lose focus, after this, and the emotions within him peak as he again recalls Spock's childhood, and Spock's youthful unwillingness to obey his father. But if Picard should ever find Spock, Sarek asks that he bear him a simple message: "Tell him, Picard. . . live long. . . and. . . "

Unable to continue as the near-madness of Ben Dai Syndrome overwhelms him once more, Sarek lapses into a tormented silence, and Picard completes the message for him: ". . . Prosper."

Picard returns to the Enterprise and proceeds to the Klingon home world, where he plans to obtain a cloaked Klingon vessel from the High Council leader, Gowron. But Gowron ignores all messages from the Enterprise. As the new leader, he is quite busy rewriting recent history, and has no desire to acknowledge the help he received from the Federation. In his official version of the story, he took control with no outside assistance.

When Picard finally gets through, it is only to face some underlings whose mission is clearly to stonewall the captain. Gowron, they say, is much too busy attending to affairs of state to talk to Picard. Picard replies with a message of his own. All he really wants is a cloaked vessel, and if Gowron is too busy to lend him one, then he's certain that he can find some other Klingon to lend him one—Klingons to whom the Federation would be most grateful. This thinly veiled threat does the trick, and Gowron releases a cloaked vessel and its crew to Picard.

Meanwhile, examination of intelligence reveals that Spock has almost certainly contacted Pardek on Romulus. Pardek is considered a radical among the Romulans due to his philosophy of peaceful co-existence with other cultures, which runs counter to the expansionist imperial designs of the Romulan ruling class. Data and Picard are altered to look like Romulans in preparation for their journey.

MYSTERY IN SPACE

Geordi determines that the metal parts found in the crashed Ferengi ship are parts of a deflector device which was originally part of a decommissioned Vulcan ship, the T'Pau. (Astute TREK watchers will of course recall who this ship was named after). But the T'Pau is supposed to be in storage at the Qualtor Two space junkyard.

Data and Picard board the Klingon ship Gowron has lent them; it is under the command of Captain K'Vada. The Klingon dislikes the secrecy of the mission, and is none too happy about their destination, either. He guesses that their mission has something to do with the missing Spock, but Picard refuses to confirm this. K'Vada then escorts the pair of imitation Romulans to their Spartan quarters, which have hard panels for beds and no mattresses.

The Enterprise, now under the command of Riker, travels to Qualtor Two in order to investigate how an old Vulcan spacecraft wound up in Ferengi hands. They contact Klim Dokachine, the manager of the junkyard, who appears to be a Plaklid. He is reluctant to help them, but finally agrees to when he is charmed by Deanna Troi. They discover that the T'Pau is indeed missing. They check out another vessel in the yard, the Tripoli, and discover that it is missing as well. But supplies have been transferred to that other ship on a regular basis, and a shipment is scheduled to be beamed aboard it that very day. The bureaucratic Klim

Dokachine is incensed to discover that he's been sending materiel to an empty location in space.

The Enterprise turns off its exterior illumination and conceals itself in the junkyard among other derelict ships to await the rendezvous time when the storage tanks will be beamed over to the missing Tripoli. They believe that some unknown vessel will take the Tripoli's former position in order to make off with the shipment. In the junkyard at Qualtor Two, a ship drops out of warp and takes the Tripoli's designated position. Riker contacts this mystery ship, which responds to his hail by immediately attacking the Enterprise. The Enterprise returns fire and damages the mystery ship's phaser banks, which causes the mystery vessel to explode.

Aboard the Klingon ship, Picard receives word that Sarek has died.

THE SEARCH FOR SPOCK

Data and Picard arrive at Romulus and prepare to beam down from their concealed orbit around the planet. Picard observes that Sarek's death now obliges him to pass that information along to Spock. Spock and his father had never fully reconciled their differences over the long years of their estrangement and so Picard can only imagine how the Vulcan will receive the news.

On the planet below, some other Romulans are questioning Pardek about Picard— they already know that he is on his way, and they tell Pardek to be on the watch for him.

Data and Picard beam down into the same Romulan neighborhood where Spock was last observed by intelligence. Someone is watching them. Data and Picard see Pardek and follow him, but they are stopped at gun point and taken to a secret cave where Pardek is waiting for them. When Picard explains that he has come in search of Spock, a figure steps out from behind a wall. When this person comes into the light, he is revealed to be Spock himself, and he announces that Picard has found the one that he seeks.

It was not possible to avoid having some reaction to the opening revelation of Spock's disappearance, and the blurry image of him on Romulus that was shown to Picard. Even if there were doubts about the way the show might turn out, there was no getting around it— it was Spock. The entire situation led to a story with considerable momentum. "Unification I" practically barreled along from scene to scene, as the mystery of the stolen Vulcan ship led Riker and the Enterprise in one direction while Picard's mission led him deeper into the mystery of Spock's disappearance.

A CLOSER LOOK

"Unification I" wasn't perfect. It did veer into a bit of a cliché once Picard and Data were disguised as Romulans. The ease of their ability to do this is just a bit too convenient, perhaps, but it does, after all, serve as a useful plot device. Picard's difficulty in

obtaining assistance from Gowron was a nice touch, however. And the final scene, in which Spock finally steps forward and speaks to Picard, provides a satisfying yet tantalizing conclusion to the first half of the story: here he is— now what's going to happen?

As it turned out, not a whole lot.

HIGH EXPECTATIONS

Directed by Cliff Bole, "Unification II" concludes the story of Spock's mission to Romulus in a Michael Piller script developed from the original story by Piller and NEXT GENERATION executive producer Rick Berman.

The story picks up exactly where "Unification I" left off, as Spock begins to explain his mission to Picard. He tells the skeptical Captain of the Enterprise that his mission is not presently any concern for Starfleet to worry itself about. He explains that he is on a personal mission of peace. Picard responds to this information by describing Spock's actions as "cowboy diplomacy." Spock justifies himself by stating that he wanted to avoid any official Federation entanglement until he had made sufficient progress in his mission.

A number of Romulans are there in the secret cavern to meet with Spock and to learn more about Vulcan philosophy, and to discuss the possible reunification between the Romulans and the Vulcans. Many centuries before, the Vulcans and the Romulans had been a single race. Spock explains to Picard that he took this particular avenue of diplomacy because he did not want to risk anyone else. He still blames himself for what happened when he urged James Kirk to become involved in the original peace overture to the Klingons, many years ago. (This, of course, is a reference to STAR TREK VI—THE UNDISCOVERED COUNTRY which was released one month after "Unification" originally aired in 1991).

Data beams back up to the cloaked Klingon ship in order to attempt to find a way to pierce the Romulan communications net. Spock and Picard, meanwhile, discuss reunification and the possibility of a Vulcan peace initiative. Picard questions how strong the Romulan underground movement could be. A Romulan boy shows Spock an old book about the split with Vulcan. It is a forbidden book, and Pardek admonishes the boy for bringing it out of hiding. Pardek then tells Spock that the Proconsul, an important figure, has agreed to meet with him.

Many light years away, Riker traces the stolen Vulcan ship T'Pau to the wife of a dead smuggler— the smuggler who was running the ship that was absconding with the Tripoli's supply shipments. Riker beams down to a cantina where strange aliens converse and are entertained. Then Riker questions the smuggler's widow, Amarie, who has four arms and plays keyboards in a sort of intergalactic piano lounge. She doesn't seem to care very much that her husband is dead and is merely amused to discover that Riker was commanding the ship which

killed him. She reveals that her late husband often dealt with Omag, a fat Ferengi who frequents her establishment.

A TRAP IS SPRUNG

Pardek takes Spock to see the Proconsul Neral, who tells the Vulcan that he supports the idea of reunification. Neral explains that times are changing, and that he is willing to publicly support talks between Vulcan and Romulus. But once Spock leaves and Neral is alone, Sela, the Romulan daughter of Tasha Yar, enters his office, smiling at what she has just overheard from her hidden vantage point.

In the cavern, Picard questions the logic of the Proconsul's support of Spock's visit, and Spock is suspicious as well. But the Vulcan will still meet with Neral as planned. Picard questions the wisdom of this. Spock explains that he must pursue this course of action in order to discover whether the Romulans indeed have an ulterior motive.

Spock beams up to the Klingon ship and helps Data break in to the Romulan communications net. Spock remarks to Data that Picard has a Vulcan quality to him. He's interested in Data's desire to be more human, when the android is already remarkably like what the Vulcans spend lifetimes striving to achieve. Data asks Spock if he has any regrets over his lost humanity?

In the alien piano bar, the Ferengi, Omag, enters just as Worf is starting to sing an excerpt of Klingon opera, with the accompaniment of the four-armed Amarie. Riker beams down and questions Omag. The Ferengi is quite obnoxious, even by Ferengi standards, so Riker threatens him. Omag crumples under pressure and reveals that he stole the T'pau and delivered it to a location near the Neutral Zone. Riker reports this new information to Picard, and they plan a rendezvous.

Picard and Data beam down to meet with Spock when the Romulan treachery is finally revealed. A group of Romulans, led by Sela, captures them in the secret cavern. Spock correctly deduces that Pardek is the traitor, as no one else would have had access to enough information to set them up.

THE FINAL TOUCH

The Romulans plan to use the unification movement as a decoy in their plan to conquer Vulcan and thus achieve reunification in their own way. Sela reveals that she has written a speech for Spock to read, in which he will state that a peace envoy is on the way to Vulcan, when in fact the three stolen Vulcan ships— the T'Pau among them— will contain a Romulan invasion force which will seize control before anyone can stop them. Spock refuses to cooperate. He knows that, logically enough, she will kill him and the two Enterprise officers anyway, so there is no need to give in to her coercive threats. This prompts Sela to remark how much she hates Vulcans. She then reveals that she has no need for Spock's cooperation anyway, as a

hologram of the ambassador will serve just as well.

The Enterprise detects the three Vulcan ships en route to Vulcan from the Neutral Zone. Suspicious of this, Riker moves in to investigate this highly irregular situation.

Meanwhile, back on Romulus, Sela returns to her office only to discover that her three prisoners are nowhere to be found. In reality, they are still there, but Data has managed to reprogram the hologram by breaking into the Romulan computer system. The hologram now presents the illusion of an empty office. Emerging from this highly effective concealment, they capture Sela and turn the tables.

A fake distress call almost succeeds in luring the enterprise away from the mysterious Vulcan ships. But just in the nick of time, a message from Spock reveals that the ships really contain the Romulan invasion forces. As Picard, Spock and Data make good their escape, Data knocks out their former captor by using the Vulcan neck pinch.

Their plan revealed, the Romulans take drastic action. A cloaked ship which has been accompanying the Vulcan vessels decloaks and destroys the entire invasion force to prevent their capture.

Spock chooses to remain on Romulus in hiding to help the Romulan underground. Before Picard leaves, Spock mind-melds with him to access Sarek's final message for his son. Spock reveals that he and his father had never melded during Sarek's lifetime. The sadness Spock feels is apparent on the face of the otherwise stoic Vulcan.

UNFINISHED MISSION

Spock's mission seems a noble one, and promises to be a fascinating and lifelong task for him. As a part of overall STAR TREK history, it certainly provides a satisfying fate for Spock.

Unfortunately, the depiction of these events proved to be a bit anticlimactic. The plotline following Riker and the Enterprise was more entertaining than the Spock/Picard/Data storyline. At the very least, the first public performance of Klingon opera, however brief, was certainly a great deal more amusing than the extended tete-a-tete between Data and Spock.

Part of the problem here may have been that the script took Spock much too seriously. Once they'd spent so much money getting Leonard Nimoy to appear on the show, it seemed as if they could think of nothing better to do with him than to treat him as some sort of icon, and failed to write any truly interesting scenes for him. Nimoy himself seems remarkably dour and uninvolved in the proceedings. Perhaps this was his take on the older, wiser Spock, but it almost seems like he was just waiting to wrap up his final shift on the job of playing Spock.

The scene in which Spock and Data work together while we're supposed to see the parallels between the two characters seemed forced, as if belaboring the obvious, and Picard's

scenes with Spock were talky and portentous. Despite its shortcomings, "Unification II" did deliver Spock as promised, and carried his history forward into the time of THE NEXT GENERATION. Only the realization of that history left a bit to be desired.

Since the "Unification" series, Vulcans have again been relegated to the occasional incidental appearance. But perhaps in time a more extensive use of the Vulcan race may be seen in future episodes of STAR TREK: THE NEXT GENERATION.

CHAPTER 8

David Gerrold saw Wesley Crusher as a character that "does not get into trouble every week, (but who) does not solve problems every week." Wil Wheaton, here seen in a 1988 photo, brought the role to life.

Photo credit: James Smeal ©1998 Ron Galella Ltd.

Gates McFadden at the Paramount Studio 25th Anniversary of Star Trek Celebration on June 6, 1991.

Photo credit: Albert Ortega, ©1998 Ron Galella Ltd.

It's sometimes hard to learn what really went on during the early formative months of the creation of a TV series, but well known writers who went on the record at the time with public statements revealed how things changed from day to day even before a single episode was ever shot.

CHAPTER 8
THE OLD GUARD LEAVES EARLY: THUNDER ON THE HORIZON

By Carl Martin

In early 1988, development was already underway for STAR TREK: THE NEXT GENERATION. While some diehard TREK fans refused to see this as anything but an unwarranted encroachment on their beloved preserve, more open minded fans of the original series were inclined to reserve judgment until THE NEXT GENERATION was available for viewing. One thing that undoubtedly set many such minds at ease was the fact that two writers from the classic STAR TREK television show were actively involved in the development of the new series.

D.C. FONTANA AND STAR TREK FIND EACH OTHER

The first of these writers, and the one with the more extensive background in STAR TREK, was D.C. Fontana. Dorothy Fontana had broken into writing for television at about the time that Gene Roddenberry's career was picking up steam in the early sixties. Her first script sale was for THE TALL MAN, a short-lived series (1960-62) about Deputy Sheriff Pat Garrett (Barry Sullivan) and his troublesome friend Billy "The Kid" Bonney (Clu Gulager). The series led Bonney deeper and deeper into crime, but never reached the final, fatal confrontation between the two men which history records. Fontana's television writing debut was the script for an early episode in this series, entitled "A Bounty For Billy."

Prior to this, Fontana had been the production secretary for the company producing the series. "A Bounty For Billy" was the first time that lines written by Fontana would be spoken by a young actor whose career would later be inextricably linked with her own. Leonard Nimoy appeared in "A Bounty For Billy" as Deputy Johnny Swift, an impetuous young lawman.

THE TALL MAN's producer, Samuel A. Peeples, himself a future STAR TREK writer, was so impressed by Nimoy's approach to the character that he brought him back in the same role in a 1961 episode, "A Gun Is For Killing." This two-time role would be the closest thing to a continuing television role for Leonard Nimoy until 1966.

Soon enough, Dorothy Fontana wound up working with Gene Roddenberry on his short-lived series, THE LIEUTENANT, which ran for twenty-nine episodes in the 1963-1964 season. By the time this ambitious dramatic series went off the air, Roddenberry was already investing a great deal of effort in another series, one which he described as "Wagon Train in space." This, of course, was STAR TREK, and Fontana was involved in the series from the very beginning, serving as story editor as well as a contributor of scripts.

The second episode of STAR TREK, "Charlie X," was co-scripted by Fontana and Roddenberry. Fontana worked solo on the script for "Tomorrow Is Yesterday" and the second season classic "Journey To Babel." "Friday's Child," "The Enterprise Incident" and "That Which Survives" round out her scripts for the original series, the last one having been co-written with John Meredyth Lucas. During the third season of STAR TREK (when Fontana no longer served as story editor for the series), "The Enterprise Incident" inspired a bit of a negative reaction from fans who felt that the script violated many established facts about Spock.

Spock makes romance with a female Romulan commander in a most un-Vulcan manner, and lies (the notorious "Vulcan Death Grip" ruse) as well, something he is supposed to be incapable of doing. Fontana bore the brunt of fan disapproval for this blasphemy for quite some time, until the truth was revealed: Fontana's original script had been extensively re-written by other hands, and the inconsistencies which marred the final form of that episode as filmed were in no way her responsibility.

INSIDE AND OUTSIDE
STAR TREK

Fontana returned to STAR TREK briefly to co-produce the short-lived STAR TREK animated series produced by Filmation in 1973, four years after the demise of the live-action TREK. Most of this show's twenty-two episodes left a great deal to be desired, but the one true exception to this rule was the D.C. Fontana-penned "Yesteryear," which showed Spock as a boy, confronting the death of a beloved pet, while the adult Spock strives to go back in time to prevent his younger self from dying, which would alter history.

While the young Spock is saved, his beloved pet is mortally wounded saving the boy. The network, uncomfortable with this dramatic ending, wanted the script altered so that the creature would survive, in order to avoid upsetting young viewers. This, of course, would have completely undermined the dramatic focus of the story. Fortunately, Fontana fought to keep her story intact, and succeeded in doing so.

In the years between the animated STAR TREK and the debut of STAR TREK: THE NEXT GENERATION, D.C. Fontana maintained her professional writing career. Her career credits include work for THE SIX MILLION

DOLLAR MAN, THE WALTONS, BEN CASEY, HIGH CHAPARRAL, BONANZA, and many other programs. The death of the Western was a bit of a loss for Fontana, as she excelled at crafting scripts for that genre, for which she retains a great affection. But in the eighties she proved to be very successful writing regularly for the hit series DALLAS.

Throughout all the years since THE LIEUTENANT, Fontana and Gene Roddenberry had been both professional collaborators and good friends. Unfortunately, Roddenberry's possessive attitude about THE NEXT GENERATION, and STAR TREK in general, would result in the end of both of these relationships.

The other NEXT GENERATION writer with a strong STAR TREK background was David Gerrold, whose involvement with the classic series dated back to his first script sale, "The Trouble With Tribbles," during the second season of the original series. This also yielded a number of books by Gerrold related both to the series in general and the "Tribbles" episode in particular. Gerrold also wrote for the STAR TREK animated series and has been a prolific writer during his career, working in television and in print. His novels include THE MAN WHO FOLDED HIMSELF, DEATHBEAST, SPACE SKIMMER, YESTERDAY'S CHILDREN, WHEN HARLEY WAS ONE, A RAGE FOR REVENGE and others.

Gerrold was involved in THE NEXT GENERATION with the dual

title of Staff Writer/Consultant. He began working in those capacities on October 20, 1986. D.C. Fontana's involvement with STAR TREK: THE NEXT GENERATION found her reprising, in essence, her role for the original series— and then some. Officially, she was an Associate Producer for THE NEXT GENERATION, specifically the Associate Producer in charge of the writing of the show, working with Executive Producer Gene Roddenberry to coordinate all the scripts. She assumed her official title on December 22, 1986, although she had actually been involved in creative discussions regarding the show at a much earlier date.

EARLY CHARACTER CONCEPTS

In February of 1987, D.C. Fontana and David Gerrold appeared together on HOUR 25, a radio talk show hosted at the time by writer Harlan Ellison. There, they discussed many facets of THE NEXT GENERATION, then early in its development.

For instance, Tasha Yar had been written in as a character just the day before that interview, replacing an earlier female Security Chief of Hispanic background. Data's name was not yet pronounced as it is now (Day-tuh) but with a short 'a' in the first syllable (Dah-ta). They referred to a character named Sternhagen who was being considered as a recurring,

but not regular, character. All that was revealed was that Sternhagen was a female character in her fifties, a brilliant woman who had already had one remarkable career and had now moved on to a new one. Neither Gerrold nor Fontana revealed what either of those careers might have been, and so Sternhagen, who never made it to the final version of THE NEXT GENERATION, must remain a mystery.

At this point, the time setting for THE NEXT GENERATION was placed by Fontana as being about one hundred years after the events of STAR TREK IV: THE VOYAGE HOME. This was later trimmed by at least twenty-five years, although it has never been clearly stated to the public exactly what event in STAR TREK's back history it is that THE NEXT GENERATION is seventy five years after. (Matters would later be confused by rumors that STAR TREK VI: THE UNDISCOVERED COUNTRY would end with Spock's wedding, with Jean-Luc Picard in attendance.

Even though this movie obviously took place a good deal later than STAR TREK V, it still would have placed its action only about thirty-five years or so before that of THE NEXT GENERATION, assuming that Picard was fifty-five years of age at the inception of the new series, as David Gerrold in fact stated at this time. This was too close, and the wedding rumor proved to be unfounded anyway).

Fontana mused that Kirk,

McCoy, Spock, Scotty et al would be rather old by this point, although there was no indication that any of these characters would be appearing on the new show. Fontana in fact felt that this would be highly unlikely, stressing that THE NEXT GENERATION would be an all-new show with all-new characters and a brand new version of the Enterprise, bigger than any previous model. Fontana also commented that the old aliens from STAR TREK: Vulcans, Romulans and Klingons, would not be featured on THE NEXT GENERATION, although Vulcans would probably be glimpsed in the background from time to time. From this it is clear that Worf had not yet been added to the cast of the series. No actors had been found to fill any of the already-established character roles at that time either.

CRAFTING THE NEXT GENERATION

Gerrold and Fontana's informal chat with Ellison revealed that THE NEXT GENERATION was just beginning to take the shape we now recognize, if only vaguely. Jean-Luc Picard was solidly established as the captain of the new Enterprise, but this had only been written in stone for about half a day at that point, and still could have changed before the show went into production. That details about this character were still being hammered out is fairly obvious from Fontana's remark that Picard would be called "Luc" for short. In six years, of course, even those who are on a first-name basis with Picard have never dared to split the hyphen!

Gerrold detailed how the captain's job had been divided, with Picard as the strategic captain who stays on the ship while his tactical captain, Will Riker, leads the Away Team (although that phrase had not yet been coined as Gerrold referred to it as the "contact team"). This, of course, makes more sense than the way Kirk used to run things and in fact coincides with centuries of military tradition. In fact, Gerrold claimed that Picard had been the man behind this policy, which could be true even though it has never been explicitly referred to in the series. What wasn't mentioned in this context was another reason that Roddenberry had split the captaincy: he was hoping to avoid any risk of having the actor playing the captain turn out to be another scene-stealing, line-swiping Bill Shatner!

The three main female characters; Dr. Crusher, Deanna Troi and Natasha Yar, were also already down on paper, although a surname for Tasha had not yet been established. (Ellison could not help but note that he would never go to a doctor with a name like Crusher!) Deanna Troi's appearance had not yet been worked out, although Fontana seemed to feel that some sort of alien makeup would be used for the character. (In fact, the final look involved little more than dark contact lenses and funny hair).

One story idea then under consideration for Deanna Troi would involve the fact that her empathic talent was not always precise: a feeling she believed she was receiving from one character would have in fact been coming from someone else and somehow reflecting off the first person.

Geordi LaForge was also already established as a character, but his prosthetic vision device had not yet been designed, and the two writers were uncertain as to how it would appear. They were not even certain as to whether or not the device would cover LaForge's eyes. When a listener called in to the show and asked if Geordi would wear something like the X-Man comic book character Cyclops wore, Gerrold was fairly certain that Geordi's eyes would not be covered.

IDEAS THAT CHANGED

As for Wesley Crusher, Gerrold made an interesting statement about that character: "He does not get into trouble every week, he does not solve problems for us every week." Was Gerrold already out of the loop at this point? During the first season of THE NEXT GENERATION it would have seemed that the exact opposite of Gerrold's statement was the truth!

At the time of this radio conversation, the premiere episode of THE NEXT GENERATION was already slated to run two hours, but at this point it had been written by only one writer: D.C. Fontana. This, of

course, would change by the fall of 1987.

Gerrold believed, at this point, that Paramount had already sold the unproduced series to something in the vicinity of one hundred and twenty markets. Stations which could not meet the per-episode cost for THE NEXT GENERATIONS had an innovative second option: they could, if they chose, simply give commercial time during the show's time slot to Paramount, who would then take care of the advertising themselves. This was at a time when the market was leaving a lot of syndicated shows high and dry. The STAR TREK name was so strong a draw that the series sold when most others did not.

At the time of the HOUR 25 interview, THE NEXT GENERATION was already slated to produce a total of twenty-six hours of programs: twenty-five episodes when you take into account the two-hour premiere. Twelve scripts were already in development, although not all of those were destined to make it to the television screen.

The design of the new series was still pretty much up in the air, but Rick Sternbach and Michael Okuda were already on the jobs they still hold today, so that question was well on its way to being resolved.

When a caller wondered why the Captain of the new Enterprise could not be a woman, Gerrold revealed that the possibility had been considered. Roddenberry apparently felt that having two male leads gave him better dramatic possibilities, and would avoid the romantic expectations that would probably otherwise arise, unbidden, from having a woman in a lead role. Audiences, or at least television executives, can't have such a situation without demanding some sort of sexual tension.

Gerrold stated, in response to Ellison's question about the possible presence of gay characters on the ship, that Gene Roddenberry had considered the possibility and had also committed to working up an episode on that theme at some point in the future. (The inherent vagueness of that way of putting it would prove to be fairly prophetic). Another episode in the works, according to Fontana, would have dealt with the AIDS crisis, at least on a thematic level.

THUNDER ON THE HORIZON

David Gerrold, whose official title was that of Staff Writer/Consultant, parted company with STAR TREK: THE NEXT GENERATION in March 1987, a mere month after appearing on the radio promoting the forthcoming series. Gerrold had a number of complaints. Somewhat reticent about these to the public at the time, Gerrold maintained later that his departure was concerned primarily with unfulfilled promises, and unrelated to his failure to get a STAR TREK episode produced with a somewhat gay-themed story. This had been touched on during the radio

interview, but it was obvious that Roddenberry had waffled on his commitment to the idea. Some claimed that Gerrold's later comments regarding the series and relation to it were merely sour grapes, and that there was nothing unusual about writers dropping out of programs, especially new programs that were still getting established.

Gerrold himself observed, however, that the high turnover rate of the various writers who were involved in the inception of STAR TREK: THE NEXT GENERATION was not that common for new shows in Hollywood, an opinion strengthened by his two decades of close-hand observation of the television business and its treatment of writers.

Of course, Gerrold would later be quite vocal about THE NEXT GENERATION's failure to address sexual issues in a clear-headed, adult manner. As can clearly be seen in the following description of two versions of the same unproduced script, even a low-key attempt to introduce gay characters to the STAR TREK universe would not sit well with Roddenberry or others. For all of STAR TREK's high handed protestations of political correctness regarding a liberal, humanistic viewpoint, sexual politics, whether with regard to women or to sexual minorities, would be a blind spot for Roddenberry and his heirs on THE NEXT GENERATION.

THE UNSEEN
NEXT GENERATION

Gerrold's original script for "Blood And Fire" involved the Enterprise in investigating a distress call from the Copernicus, a Federation research vessel. An Away Team beams over to the Copernicus; the team consists of Riker, Tasha, Geordi and three male characters named Freeman, Eakins and Hodel. (In an interesting note, this early NEXT GENERATION script features Worf as the Transporter Chief). When the Away Team beams to the Copernicus, they encounter a sparkling cloud of the sort familiar on the old show, barely perceptible at first but quickly becoming more obvious. As Hodel and Eakins try to reactivate a computer console, Hodel, obviously a busybody, muses on the relationship between Eakins and Freeman; they've been together for two years, ever since Starfleet Academy, says Eakins.

Life readings on the ship are weak, and the mummified body of a crew member, utterly devoid of blood, is found. A surviving crew member, hysterical, is also found, but he grabs a phaser and kills himself. As he disappears, more of the red and gold particles are seen. Meanwhile, Data's researches on the Enterprise have revealed that the strange particles are plasmasites, better known as Regulian bloodworms.

This is such a vile and incurable disease that Starfleet regulations completely forbid any attempt to rescue anyone infected. An intense series of shocks ensues, as Hodel is attacked by the worms and Eakins must decide to kill the man in order to end his hellish torments. The rest of the Away Team is eventually beamed away to the Copernicus cargo bay, and quarantined inside a slowly weakening repulsor field along with a handful of Copernicus survivors, including one named Yarell. Yarell was on a Federation-sanctioned investigation onto whether or not the bloodworms could be neutralized once they'd infested a human host.

Beverly Crusher beams over to the Copernicus despite Captain Picard's objections. Some Enterprise personnel express fear that the contagion will spread to their ship, a sentiment quickly put in its place by Picard. Crusher, meanwhile, intends to remove everyone's blood and replace it with transfusions, a plan somewhat hampered by a shortage of artificial blood.

A blood drive is organized on the Enterprise. As the transfusions proceed, the Copernicus officers are beamed over to the Enterprise, where Picard suspects that the bloodworm research may have potential military misapplications.

Eventually, Riker, Eakins and Freeman are the last to go. With the repulsor field collapsing, Freeman forces the other two men to beam back to the Enterprise. The field collapses; sensors indicate that Freeman is still infected, and Freeman kills himself with a phaser blast.

Picard wants to destroy the Copernicus, but that might simply release the bloodworms into space. Then it is discovered that the Copernicus is on a course into Ferengi territory. Yarell, who has planned to destroy the Ferengi with the disease, pulls out a vial of bloodworms that he will release if Picard interferes. Eakins pulls a phaser on Yarell. Yarell's subordinate, Blodgett, grabs the vial and swallows the bloodworms! He then takes an experimental cure devised by Dr. Crusher and is beamed back to the Copernicus, where Crusher's theory is proven correct and the bloodworms metamorphose into a beautiful, non lethal life form, with Blodgett sacrificing his life in the process.

THE STORY BEHIND THE STORY

This script was David Gerrold's commentary on AIDS. It certainly was no more heavy handed than any of the other STAR TREK takes on current issues. It also was a pretty action-packed story. Gerrold's depiction of a Federation where everyone was equal and treated as such, regardless of anything, sexual preferences included, seems perfectly in keeping with the whole open-minded viewpoint of the series. But it was obviously not in keeping with current notions of marketability. Gerrold himself eventually made his drafts of "Blood and Fire" publicly

available, and had a few words regarding it at a public appearance.

"What I wanted to do was deal with Regulan bloodworms," he explained, "because we had mentioned them in "The Trouble With Tribbles.

"People were always asking me about them, but who knows what a Regulan bloodworm is? At that particular time there was a lot in the news about the AIDS panic and people not donating blood. Blood donorship was a major issue for me and always has been, and to hear that donorship was down because of fear of AIDS exposure, I wanted to do a story where at some point maybe everybody on the Enterprise must roll up their sleeves to donate blood to save the lives of some of their crew members. So that was floating around in my head. Also, we had a discussion of whether or not we could use Mike Minor as our art director. Unfortunately, Mike was very sick with AIDS at the time and has since passed away, which is a great loss to us."

Gerrold added, "In November of 1986, we all— Gene [Roddenberry] and I, George Takei, Robin Curtis and some others— were at a convention in Boston. "It was a twentieth anniversary [STAR TREK] celebration, and they had invited us all before they knew there was going to be a STAR TREK: THE NEXT GENERATION, so we all went out there and they were thrilled, because we were able to talk about what we planned to do on the new show, and they were very excited.

"There is apparently a gay science fiction club in Boston and they said, 'Gene, we've always had, on STAR TREK in the past, minorities clearly represented, isn't it time we had a gay crewmember on the Enterprise?'

"He said, 'You're probably right, sooner or later we'll have to address the issue and I'll have to give serious thought to it.' I thought, 'Okay, fine,' because I was sitting at the back taking notes. Whatever Gene said was going to be policy. We came back to Los Angeles and I'm still making notes for the bible and other things, and we're at a meeting with Eddie Milkis, Bob Justman, John D.F. Black, Gene and myself, and Gene said, 'We should probably have a gay character on STAR TREK. We seriously have to be willing to address the issue.' So I said, 'Okay, now I know [that] Gene seriously meant what he said in Boston, and I know that that's story material we could do.

CONCEPT TO CONCEPT

"At that time I felt very positive, because by saying we could do that kind of story, Gene was also indicating a willingness to do a whole range of story material. As a writer I was excited, not just by that particular idea, but by the whole range of story ideas that were available. All of this [was] floating around in my head. I wanted to do a story that somehow acknowledged the AIDS fear, something about blood

donorship, and I started blocking out a story called "Blood And Fire" about Regulan bloodworms. Where it started was with the idea that we find a ship that has been infected, and if you have a starship that is infected, what do you do without bringing the infection to your ship? I thought we should make it [such] a really horrendous thing that there's a standing Starfleet order that when you run into a ship that's infected with bloodworms, the order is to destroy that ship immediately.

"In the first few stories written we saw that they were a little soft and there wasn't much action, and to balance that I wanted to do a show that had a lot of hard action and adventure in it. So the idea [was] that they could find another ship infected with the bloodworms and have a major problem, and to make it even more serious, first the Away Team beams over and then they find out [that] the ship is infected with bloodworms.

"That's where I started; then I worked out the life cycle of the bloodworms, that they grow in your blood until they reach a certain point and then, like malaria, they explode and start looking for new flesh. It was a very graphic kind of suggestion. I had a lot of fun with it, Dorothy [Fontana] liked it and Herb Wright loved it, saying that it was the kind of story we needed to do."

As for the scene suggesting a homosexual relationship between Freeman and Eakins, Gerrold stated: "I wrote that in a way to acknowledge the contribution that gay people have made to the show and acknowledge they were all taking a large part of the burden for the AIDS epidemic, because this story was an AIDS allegory. Then we [dealt] with blood donation.

"When I finished ["Blood and Fire"] I felt that it represented some of the best writing I'd ever done for television, and I thought it could be a better episode than "The Trouble With Tribbles." I turned it in, and went off on the first STAR TREK cruise, and got a telegram from Gene that said 'Everyone loved your script, have a great cruise.' When I got back I found that the script was not going to be shot. I was told that Gene's lawyer [Leonard Maizlish] did not like the script and felt that this was not a good episode, and so on his advice, it seems, the script was canceled. That's what I was told by someone who was in a position to know. I don't have any proof in writing, so I have to qualify it by saying [that] someone told me. So, it was canceled for reasons that had nothing to do with its quality. It was just put on a shelf. I was very hurt and very upset about it, and the only way I can share it is to allow [the public] decide if this would have been a good STAR TREK episode."

REWRITTEN TO DEATH

A second draft of "Blood and Fire," rewritten by Herb Wright and retitled "Blood and Ice," kept the basic adventure plot but dropped Gerrold's character material and the AIDS allegory as well. In this version, people who died of the bloodworm disease became zombies and chased the Enterprise Away Team around the Copernicus! It, too, was never filmed. (To show how early on this was in the development of THE NEXT GENERATION, "Blood and Ice" also featured a Romulan as part of the Enterprise crew!).

This, then, was one of the reasons that David Gerrold left THE NEXT GENERATION so early in the development stage: it had become clear to him that Gene Roddenberry, despite his noble promises of depicting a truly equal-opportunity future, still had his prejudices firmly rooted in the 20th Century. But that was not all. Even more crucial to Gerrold's departure was Roddenberry's arbitrary dismissal of Gerrold's input to the series, and his failure to recognize Gerrold's conceptual contributions to the series early in its development stages by granting him a screen credit for co-development.

The other STAR TREK veteran whose presence gave credibility to THE NEXT GENERATION would leave for almost identical reasons, although she would stay with production long enough to see the show get off the ground. In October of 1987, D.C. Fontana, whose presence had been intended to serve as a vitally important link between the STAR TREK of the sixties and its eighties offspring, also departed, unhappy with Roddenberry's tampering with her work, among other things.

Fontana had been distressed by the fashion in which her original "Encounter at Farpoint" script had been grafted onto Roddenberry's familiar "humanity-on-trial" plot featuring the entity known as "Q" (John DeLancie), which bore more than a passing resemblance to the original series' episode "The Squire of Gothos." Ultimately, Fontana would only contribute four scripts to the series, and all of these would be rewritten extensively by Roddenberry.

The crux of the matter for both of these writers was not simply anger at having their scripts rewritten, or the dismissal of themes that they regarded as important and worthy of depiction. Both Dorothy Fontana and David Gerrold also felt, with considerable justification, that they had contributed a great deal to the development of the series concept for STAR TREK: THE NEXT GENERATION, and had not received the credit which should have been their due. Roddenberry certainly never admitted to any such contribution from Fontana or Gerrold. In fact, of Gerrold, he commented that "I had [Gerrold] on staff for many, many months, [and] he never wrote an episode we could shoot."

Other voices at Paramount also alleged that Gerrold was abrasive and counter-productive during the start-up of the series, something flatly denied by Gerrold and by D. C. Fontana as well. They both filed grievances against Paramount with the Writer's Guild.

The truth of the matter, however, would seem to lie with these two fine writers. After all, Paramount would eventually reach a settlement with each of them, for an undisclosed amount of money. D.C. Fontana and David Gerrold may have created more of STAR TREK: THE NEXT GENERATION than they will ever be given any official credit for, but for Paramount and Gene Roddenberry it was obviously more important to propagate Roddenberry's pet myth of himself as a solo creator, a demurrage who acknowledges no one's handiwork but his own, and was perfectly willing to take credit that was not entirely his own, than it was to openly acknowledge the truth.

Marina Sirtis and her husband, Michael Lambert, on March 13, 1993
as the Starlight Foundation honored Arsenio Hall and Star Trek: The Next Generation.

CHAPTER 9

Levar Burton at UCLA's Royce Hall Eco Conference in 1991.

Photo credit: Albert Ortega, ©1991 Ron Galella Ltd.

Marina Sirtis at the Hotel Nikko Grand Open Feb. 10, 1992.

Photo credit: James Smeal, ©1992 Ron Galella Ltd.

What impact does traditional organized religion have on life in the 24th century? On STAR TREK it seems that only primitive societies still cling to the beliefs surrounding the concept of a supreme being. While that's certainly the universe that Gene Roddenberry created, is it an honestly believable one?

CHAPTER 9

WATCHING THE WATCHERS: RELIGION IN THE RODDENBERRY UNIVERSE

By Bill Renouvier

Religion and science fiction: the intersection between the two has led to many important literary works over the years, from Ursula LeGuin's anthropological considerations to Philip K. Dick's metaphysical and moral obsessions. From James Blish's Catholic conscience to C.S. Lewis' out-and-out Christian allegory, and many, many more. Many writers have simply invented their own religions for fictional purposes— or for entirely different purposes, in the case of L. Ron Hubbard.

The religious aspect of human experience is so vast and varied that one doesn't really need to look very far for something to inspire an interesting science fiction idea. Christianity alone has so many subdivisions and factions that one hardly even needs to look elsewhere— Philip K. Dick's short story "Rautavaara's Case" took as its basis the simple notion that an alien race rescuing some spacewrecked humans might take the Eucharistic meaning of "eating the body and blood of Christ" a bit too literally, with grim results. Islam, Buddhism and its various forms, Hinduism in its polytheistic splendor, and the many dead religions and heresies of human history can provide many such inspirations. A creative mind need not subscribe to any given set of beliefs in order to use it as a springboard for compelling, thought-inducing literature. One can get inside a religion or attack it from without, and both techniques have yielded fertile fictional results.

The question, then, is this: if religion is such a ready-made source for science fiction source material, why has the treatment of the subject in STAR TREK and THE NEXT GENERATION been so limited? A prime example to focus on is the NEXT GENERATION episode "Who Watches The Watchers?" This is a very good episode as it tells a good story and tells it well. But the underlying attitude towards religion, although a valid one, is the same one that has consistently undermined any really interesting use of religious concepts in STAR TREK, the TREK movies, THE NEXT GENERATION, or even DEEP SPACE NINE. DEEP SPACE NINE, which Roddenberry reportedly had no real hand in developing, attempts to use the Bajoran religion as a cornerstone of the show's background, but which obviously has no idea of how to construct a fictional religion. The crux of the matter lies in Gene Roddenberry's attitude towards religion: utter rejection.

The author of this piece, like Roddenberry, saw enough nonsense perpetrated in the name of religion in his youth to inspire him to back out of the religious beliefs he was raised with. It seems that Roddenberry, through his utter unwillingness to recognize the importance of religion to many cultures, or any cultures, and his failure to consider the complexity of the issue, was never really able to incorporate religious ideas into his STAR TREK universe with any degree of success.

WHEN MEN BECOME GODS

"Who Watches The Watchers," written by Richard Manning and Hans Beimler, epitomizes Roddenberry's take on the matter of religion, and stands as perhaps the best statement of his attitude in fictional form. A synopsis of the episode is thus presented for examination as it clearly shows the philosophy of the creator of this fictional universe.

An anthropological team observing the proto-Vulcan inhabitants of Mentaka-III experiences a power failure in its holographically concealed station, located in a rock face above the Mentakan village that is the focus of their survey. One of the team members, Palmer, is thrown clear of the area by an ensuing explosion. The arrival of an Away Team sent from the Enterprise to rescue the scientists coincides with the discovery of the post by two of the Mentakan villagers.

The Mentakans possess a culture that is technologically on a level with the Bronze Age of Earth's prehistory, but they have a somewhat unusual quality in that they have intentionally discarded all superstitions and religion generations before. These, their ancestors reasoned, added nothing but unnecessary complications to the business of living.

But things become rather complicated when the outpost is found by Liko and his daughter. While the young woman, Oji, watches, her father climbs up to peer into the observation post, only to be shocked by some residual energy left after the explosion. Stunned, he falls a great distance to the ground below, and is seriously injured. The Away Team inside the post happens to include Dr. Crusher, and she climbs down to help the man. In order to save his life, she beams up to the Enterprise with him, an act which is observed by Oji, hiding nearby.

A GOD NAMED PICARD

Against all expectations, Liko awakens while on board the Enterprise. This is momentary, but it is long enough for him to realize the strangeness of his surroundings, and to see Picard, who is obviously the being-in-charge. Crusher tries to erase the memory of the experience from Liko's mind using the technique developed by Dr. Pulaski (in the episode "Pen Pals"), but it does not work, and when Liko awakens back on Mentaka, he believes that he has had a mystical experience in which he has seen one of the gods out of his people's ancient legends.

In order to seek out Palmer, the missing scientist, Deanna Troi and Will Riker are surgically altered to resemble Mentakans. They are outfitted with implanted transmitters, and beamed down to the planet. They walk into the village, where they are welcomed by the community, just as Liko is regaling his people with an account of his experience, of the miraculous intervention which brought him back to life, and of the god he calls "The Picard." This inspires an exchange of quizzical glances between Riker and Troi. Something has obviously gone very, very wrong here.

The other villagers are skeptical, especially the village leader, a woman named Nouria. Other villagers soon arrive with the injured Palmer in tow. Liko surmises that Palmer is a servant who has failed The Picard and has been cast out by the god. Perhaps they can win the good will of The Picard by punishing Palmer. While the villagers debate this, Troi slips out of the meeting-place, and returns claiming to have seen another stranger nearby. When the villagers go out to investigate, Riker makes off with the injured Palmer, only to be pursued by a bow-wielding Mentakan. He eludes this pursuer just long enough to beam up unobserved, along with Palmer.

But all is not well, for the Mentakans, being intelligent, link Troi's ruse with the escape of the prisoner, and take her prisoner.

WHEN GODS BLEED

Picard is in a quandary. There seems to be no way to rescue Deanna without compromising the Prime Directive. Picard takes a radical course of action: he beams Nouria, the village leader, up to the Enterprise to explain the truth to her and dispel the misconception that he is a god. She readily grasps the concept that there are societies throughout the universe that have reached different levels of social and technological development, and that there is nothing divine or supernatural about Picard, but she still believes that he has the power to bring the dead back to life. To prove that this is also not true, Picard takes Nouria to Sickbay, where one of the injured scientists is dying. Nouria witnesses this death, which Picard cannot prevent, and is now completely convinced that what Picard says it true.

Picard returns to the planet with Nouria, only to come face-to-face with the unstable Liko, who begs for the return of his dead wife. Liko tries to prove Picard's powers by shooting him with an arrow. Picard bravely stands his ground. Fortunately, Liko's daughter Oji pushes him and throws his aim off. The arrow catches Picard in the shoulder rather than in any vital organs. He bleeds, however, and this finally convinces Liko that Picard is not a god.

Picard meets with the Mentakan villagers one more time, and explains the Prime Directive to them. He tells them he could help them advance their culture technologically, but this would violate the Directive and throw the natural development of their society off course, perhaps with disastrous results. They understand and send him off with a fond farewell. Picard is suitably impressed with their intelligence as well as their determination to persevere, and as the episode ends he says that he is certain that the Mentakans will be a culture that will reach space in due time.

RELIGION AS SLEIGHT OF HAND

While this is a good story, which deals as much with the dangers of tampering with another society as much as it does with religion, it is fairly consistent with other takes on religion in the Roddenberry universe. On the original STAR TREK, "The Apple" is a prime example: a godlike computer controls the lives of everyone on a planet, and Kirk must show them that they're living a lie. In THE NEXT GENERATION, this was echoed in the episode "Justice." Again, a computer provides to the needs of a fairly unthinking culture, although Picard at least has the decency not to upset the apple cart.

Another take on this idea was also seen in the episode "Devil's Due," in which a planet's ancient Faust legend seems to come true, until it is revealed that it is the work of an intergalactic thief. The Klingon religion got a similar treatment quite recently when an ancient hero of Klingon religion returned to save the Empire. It turns out he is a clone created by the priests in an effort to dupe their followers. In the Roddenberry universe, religion is almost always treated as being a dupe or a con.

What is the origin of this entire attitude? Before the nineteenth century, religion and science were not generally at odds, although religious organizations were of course always quick to suppress ideas that threatened the party line. The

Catholic church's massacre of the Albigensians in the twelfth century and their treatment of Galileo were in many ways the same reflective, protective gesture of any vested authority. But then, science had not developed that far in Galileo's time; his persecution can be seen as one of its birth pangs.

Issues really heated up in the nineteenth century when advances in archaeology, geology and the development of evolutionary theory began to present a threat to long-standing Western religious belief— while a Hindu or a Buddhist of the time would probably never have had the problem with Darwin's ideas that Christians did. In time, however, this dialogue led to a number of concessions by religious figures, and opened the way to non-literal interpretations of the Bible which concentrated on the spiritual and ethical ideas without expecting anyone to believe the more far fetched statements in scripture. Of course, there has always been a fundamentalist backlash against that trend; and, on the other hand, there has always remained an anti-religious contingent in the scientific community.

This, in turn, fed into the burgeoning field of science fiction in the thirties. Many science fiction writers had an attitude similar to Roddenberry's, but they often produced more interesting tales out of it, even if their stance was one of opposition. Dr. Isaac Asimov was certainly not a religious man, but that never kept him from treating the Bible seriously as a statement of humanity's struggle to understand their universe, and his hundreds of books contain a number of volumes on the subject in the non-fiction category.

WHAT GENE SAID

In approaching "Who Watches The Watchers," episode director Robert Wiemer was a bit concerned that the show's message might offend some viewers. This never seemed to be the case. Instead, it turned out to be a gripping story where Picard found himself in the awkward position of being considered a god by some Mentakans when they discovered a Federation observation post near their village, and witnessed such seeming miracles as Starfleet personnel disappearing into thin air.

Of course, this was a pet issue of Gene's. "I've always thought," said Roddenberry, "that if we did not have supernatural explanations for all the things [that] we might not understand right away, this is the way we would be, like the people on that planet." (The Mentakans had actually discarded a supernatural viewpoint centuries before but some of them tried to turn back to it when confronted with the seemingly inexplicable 'powers' of Picard and crew). Roddenberry further detailed his feelings on this subject:

"I was born into a 'supernatural' world in which all my people— my family—usually said, 'That is because God willed it,' or gave other supernatural explanations for whatever happened. When you confront those statements on their own, they just don't make sense. They are clearly wrong. You need a certain amount of proof to accept anything, and that proof was not forthcoming to support those statements."

Roddenberry was rather disappointed at the lack of public response to "Who Watches The Watchers," having hoped, perhaps, to generate some degree of controversy over it, if not to utterly convert viewers outright to his ultrarational but grossly oversimplified views on the subject. He didn't seem to realize that the people who would enter this debate in earnest, the fundamentalist Christian right, probably don't watch THE NEXT GENERATION anyway.

"It is a source of considerable amusement to me," Roddenberry claimed, "that we can do shows like this and on various other subjects, large and small, and get little or no public reaction. If these things were to be done on Broadway or in motion pictures, they would have stunned audiences. The audiences would have said, 'How wild, how forward, how advanced.' But because these subjects are done on a syndicated television show, in our time slot, no one really notices them."

RODDENBERRY AS PHILOSOPHER

Roddenberry discussed his views on this subject in an interview which appeared in THE HUMANIST magazine shortly before his death. He continued, "I thought several times that the world of drama would have stood up and cheered us, but no, only silence. But there is one advantage, one thing

happening: all of these episodes are brought back and rerun every year. What will happen with STAR TREK: THE NEXT GENERATION is almost identical to what happened to the original STAR TREK, as larger and larger audiences become acquainted with the program.

"The original STAR TREK audience now says, 'Hurrah, what fine shows.' This has brought us considerable pleasure that they would notice it. STAR TREK: THE NEXT GENERATION is on that same path now and more so. The time will come when the second series will attain its true stature. I just hope some of it happens while I'm still alive; I'm not jealous that I don't have praise. This happens very broadly in contacts with humans. The world is not necessarily poorer because a painter or playwright is not recognized in his or her lifetime."

A certain sense of self-importance permeates these seemingly humble words of the late Gene Roddenberry, would-be philosopher. Perhaps, in time, successive reruns of "Who Watches the Watchers" and other issue-oriented STAR TREK episodes will cause the world to sit up and take notice of Gene Roddenberry.

THE RELIGIONS OF STAR TREK

All sarcasm aside, the interesting thing about Roddenberry's stance on religion is that STAR TREK in its various forms has, while rejecting religion with one hand, always seemed to yearn for a religious experience with the other. STAR TREK—THE MOTION PICTURE is a case in point. Although V'Ger is in fact a technological artifact, and the apotheosis of Ilia and Decker is described as an "evolutionary" breakthrough, the entire sequence is approached with an almost religious fervor.

Likewise, there has always been a concerted attempt to depict alien religions in various TREK settings. The Vulcans have always been depicted as ultrarational on one hand and deeply mystical on the other. Various rituals from the Klingon culture and religion have been depicted on THE NEXT GENERATION. The problem in both these cases is that we are still left with no real idea of what the basic beliefs of either of these religions might be.

Beyond a few made-up words and some ritualistic trappings, we have no idea what's really going on with Spock or Worf in a spiritual sense. In the new DEEP SPACE NINE series, the Bajoran religion plays a major part in the plot of the pilot, but all we really see are a religious leader with a distinctive costume, a building or two, and a mystical sanctum of some sort housing a mysterious orb. But what do these people believe? All we get are outer trappings. For all we know, the religions of the Vulcans, the Klingons and the Bajorans might be exactly the same, with only cosmetic differences.

Do the shows have neither the time nor the ability to try to figure out what the true character of their fictional religions are? Are they afraid that they will offend someone if they present a fictional religion with any clearly articulated beliefs? They probably would. But wouldn't it be worth that risk to find out that the Vulcan religion was basically an atheistic one, like most forms of Buddhism, involved in personal spiritual development but not requiring any belief in any god? Wouldn't it be worth it to know that certain rites of the Vulcan religion involve some sort of bloodshed, like the royal religion of the ancient Mayans did? And wouldn't it be great to discover that Bajoran religion involved more than wearing earrings? And for that matter, do any of the humans on board the Enterprise still practice any Earth religions?

It would be ridiculous to assume that humanity had discarded all of its spiritual traditions four hundred years from now. The Christianity that Roddenberry endured in his youth might very well have faded away, but any religion with as many forms as Christianity would probably have survived in some form, and probably in many forms. While some religions, such as the varieties of Hinduism, might not transplant well into space, a religion like Buddhism would probably survive quite well. And new religions would have undoubtedly developed in four centuries and yielded at least a few durable beliefs. Unfortunately, STAR TREK: THE NEXT GENERATION and the other offshoots of Gene Roddenberry's STAR TREK universe have failed to approach the matter of religion in any creative fashion.

CHAPTER 10

Whoopi Goldberg at the 1991 Oscar Luncheon at the Beverly hills Hotel.

Photo credit: ©1991 Ron Galella Ltd.

CHAPTER 10

YESTERDAY'S ENTERPRISE: THE RETURN OF TASHA YAR

By James Van Hise

"Let's make sure history never forgets the name Enterprise."
—Jean-Luc Picard

When Denise Crosby left THE NEXT GENERATION at the end of the first season, few people were satisfied by the manner of her exit. While the Tasha Yar hologram at her funeral was an important touch, her death was meaningless as she was reduced to being treated like an expendable "red shirt" (a "red shirt" was a nameless crewmember who went along on a landing party for seemingly no other reason than to be killed).

With a regular cast of nine people, scripts could seldom concentrate on any one character. Having to split the screen among nearly a dozen people, the result was haphazard storytelling. Avoiding that, the result was a few characters getting the lion's share of attention while the others stood around saying, "Yes, sir" or "I feel great pain." Denise Crosby ultimately felt great pain at her treatment on the series and opted to leave in search of more challenging acting work.

She did not part on bad terms. She was liked as an actress but the writers just didn't know what to do with her character. In spite of the fact that the early drafts of the series premise for STAR TREK: THE NEXT GENERATION clearly show that the character of Tasha Yar was inspired by the female Marine Vasquez in the 1986 hit movie ALIENS (the character even had a Latino name before being altered to Tasha Yar), the writers just apparently weren't comfortable writing a female character as a dynamic warrior type. As a result she wasn't written as much of anything at all. Roddenberry himself rewrote the first dozen episodes, thereby demonstrating that he didn't know what to do with the character either. So Crosby got tired of showing up to do little and asked to be written out. In episode 22, "Skin Of Evil," she got her wish.

In season three the writing staff and the producers hatched a plan to bring Tasha Yar back for the kind of send off she deserved. The teleplay is by Ira Steven Behr, Richard Manning, Hans Beimler and Ronald D. Moore, based on a story by Trent Christopher Ganing and Eric A. Stillwell. When that many writers work on a script the result is usually something resembling

a collision of concepts with ideas scattered hither and yon like bodies after an accident. But in this case the meeting of the minds produced a superior result. Directed by David Carson, the guest cast consisted of Denise Crosby, Christopher McDonald, and Tricia O'Neil in a story which was both powerful and compelling.

TIME TRACKS

The episode opens in Ten Forward where Guinan introduces Worf to the pleasures of prune juice, which the Klingon pronounces "a warrior's drink." He is called to the bridge when a strange phenomenon—a temporal rift—appears in the path of the Enterprise. A Federation ship emerges from the void; as it does so, the timelines shift, and the Enterprise becomes a war vessel, for the Federation has now been fighting the Klingon Empire for the past twenty-two years.

Worf is no longer on the ship—but Tasha Yar is, never having encountered the creature Armus in "Skin of Evil." The other ship is the Enterprise-C, which vanished around the time of the failed peace talks with the Klingons.

Guinan senses that something is amiss, and tries to convince Captain Picard that the earlier Enterprise, damaged in a battle with Romulans, must go back to its own time despite its almost certain destruction. Reluctantly, Picard comes around to this view. The Enterprise-C seems to be a key factor in history, for it was actually defending a Klingon outpost from a Romulan sneak attack before its trip through time. Had it succeeded, the Klingons may have been impressed by the sacrifice of the Federation vessel, as they value honor very highly. Picard confides to the other Enterprise's captain, Rachel Garrett, that the war is going badly for the Federation— a war which has already cost four billion lives. Starfleet believes that the Federation will be forced to surrender within 6 months.

Tasha Yar becomes involved in her work with Lieutenant Castillo, an officer on the ship from the past. She also becomes increasingly aware that something is wrong with her presence on the ship because of how peculiarly Guinan looks at her. After Captain Picard holds a briefing in which he reveals Guinan's firm belief about what has happened, Tasha becomes even more concerned about her own role in the scheme of things.

Tasha goes to Guinan and asks her outright what her life was like in the alternate timeline. Guinan tells her that her death in the other timeline was senseless, "An empty death. A death without purpose." Tasha is upset by this revelation and leaves Guinan's quarters without saying anything more.

KILLED IN ACTION

Captain Garrett tells her crew the truth about what they suspect has happened, and most of them quickly volunteer to return in order to finish

the battle the Romulans began 22 years before. As the crew of the Enterprise-C is working to repair and refit their vessel for its return journey through the destabilizing rift, the two Enterprises are suddenly attacked by a Klingon ship. Captain Garrett is killed in the attack, which further hurts the capacity of the Enterprise-C to face what will confront them when they return through the rift. Tasha Yar volunteers to join Castillo on the Enterprise-C in order to gain a meaningful departure from the world. "I'd like my death to count for something." Picard agrees, realizing that all of them may well be doomed.

Tasha Yar beams over to the Enterprise-C and reports for duty. Lt. Castillo is now Captain as he is the only surviving bridge officer. When Tasha offers her services on tactical he resists, admitting that he knows he's embarking on a suicide mission. Tasha points out that the extra minutes her advanced knowledge of tactics could provide them could make the difference between a Klingon/Federation war and a lasting peace caused by their valiant sacrifice in the face of hopeless odds. Finally Castillo relents, burdened with the knowledge that the woman he loves will die at his side.

As the Enterprise-C prepares to return through the temporal rift, three more Klingon ships are detected on long distance sensors. The Klingons are on an intercept course, not even bothering to cloak their approach. The Enterprise-D is outgunned but strives to shield the Enterprise-C from attack until the other vessel can return through the rift. The Enterprise-D experiences core damage and is minutes away from a warp core breach when the Enterprise-C disappears back through the rift and the timelines are restored.

The Enterprise-D is suddenly back to normal, and Lieutenant Worf reports only a brief fluctuation in the sensor readings. Whatever was there in space is gone now. No one has any knowledge of the alternative reality just avoided, except Guinan, who joins Geordi in Ten Forward and asks him to tell her about Tasha Yar.

CREATIVE ANGST

The ending of this episode is a touching one, capturing as it does the sense of loss for Tasha Yar far better than even the extended funeral scene in "Skin Of Evil" did. One even wonders whether Guinan, perhaps, even feels some small sense of guilt over the knowledge that her actions in causing time to be corrected resulted in the second death of Tasha Yar. Although billions of lives were saved, who otherwise would have perished in the extended war, Guinan only had personal contact with a single life that she knew would be irrevocably altered. Its underlying meaning is only underscored by the fifth season revelation of what really happened to Tasha Yar when she went back in time on the Enterprise-C.

In spite of how superior the episode turned out, it was tough going all the way. The producers were under a scheduling crunch because Christmas was approaching and Whoopi Goldberg had other commitments in January which would prevent her working on THE NEXT GENERATION.

When director David Carson arrived at Paramount to begin the preproduction sessions for "Yesterday's Enterprise," he found that there wasn't even a first draft of the script finished yet, just a story outline by production assistant Eric Stillwell. This story outline, which Stillwell submitted, was the genesis for the episode and was rewritten and expanded on to create what was ultimately filmed. Because of the strength of the idea, people got behind it and did their utmost to make it work.

Carson attended a concept meeting in which the production heads and the writers discussed the script in order to reach a consensus on what they were seeking to achieve with the storyline. Since the director was not ordinarily as involved in plotting out the script this early on, Carson pushed for the altered Enterprise having very specific differences from the familiar Enterprise, rather than merely subtle differences. Some critics remarked that the result, showing a more hard-edged treatment of the characters in the altered setting, brought to mind an Enterprise very much in the tradition of the one commanded by Captain Kirk, where officers didn't always find themselves in easy agreement on the course of action to follow.

There is also an ever-present bustle of activity on this Enterprise as the crew always have something to do and somewhere to go. This Enterprise, not being a ship of peace, does not have any families aboard, and in fact Picard is amazed when Guinan suggests that this is the way it was before. And yet we do see that Wesley Crusher is still there—as a 16 year old working on the bridge. This discrepancy is never explained.

TIMESLIP

On the bridge, the ship of war versus the ship of peace alterations were signified in certain specific ways. For instance, the Captain's chair was in a more elevated position—almost like a throne rather than just a central command point. Patrick Stewart really took to this chance to play Picard with a different slant. Here, after 22 years of war with the Klingons began, Picard was a war-weary Captain facing inevitable defeat. This was far different from the usual fix of Picard as an ambassador. The altered Enterprise was also not as pristine as what we'd known. Even the crew could be seen to be more tense and alert because they knew they could be fighting for their lives at any moment. Clearly this Enterprise was a warship on alert, not a vessel of discovery and exploration.

The scene in the teaser when the Enterprise-C appears from the rift in space and the transition shows that the normal Enterprise has been altered into something different, was actually an afterthought. During editing it was pointed out that if we went from the normal Enterprise to the Enterprise-C special effect and then to the altered Enterprise crew, the audience could too easily be confused and think they were seeing the crew of the Enterprise-C as though it was an alternate universe version of our ship emerging from the rift in space. But careful editing made it clear that the Enterprise-D was the same ship and that it was everyone aboard it who had suddenly changed. By masking out Picard and having the background waver as his uniform changed, the fact of the time shift was immediately communicated.

How different this timeline is can best be exemplified in the scene when the Enterprise-D, under attack from Klingon vessels, receives a communication from a Klingon commander instructing the Enterprise to surrender, to which Picard remarks, "That will be the day."

This comes across as a bit of an inside joke as Captain Kirk never agreed to surrender the Enterprise until the 6th STAR TREK feature film, whereas Captain Picard surrendered the Enterprise in the very first episode, "Encounter At Farpoint." In fact one of the early criticisms of THE NEXT GENERATION was that Picard kept surrendering his ship.

This remains one of the most tightly written episodes, both from characterization and from a storytelling perspective. We're plunged into the altered timeline story without anyone standing around telling us what is going on. We have to pay attention and figure it out for ourselves or be completely lost until Guinan goes to Picard and confronts him with her belief about what has happened. The editing is precise and the story moves along at a breakneck pace.

THE RETURN OF TASHA YAR

Denise Crosby as Tasha Yar never had a better episode written for her character than this one. Even though she is not in every scene, we're constantly thinking about her because she's a wild card in this adventure just as much as the altered Enterprise and the Federation/Klingon war is. If the dead can be brought back to life again due to time troubles, what else might happen? Her presence, in defiance of what we know happened before, lends weight to the grim possibility of the defeat of the Federation by the Klingon Empire.

Said co-writer Ron Moore, "I've heard from time to time—'I wish you'd do some war stories.' But this is the reality of war. It's not a pretty piece, but it was a lot of fun to watch that ship move, and see Picard biting Riker's head off. I wrote a couple of different story outlines on it. Somewhere during the course of that I came up with the idea that the alternate universe would really be nasty and awful and militaristic, and that we're losing the war with the Klingons."

"Yesterday's Enterprise" presented not just a scenario which allowed the return of Tasha Yar, but it also allowed for the treatment of the

NEXT GENERATION characters in a manner which violated Roddenberry's own personal Prime Directive on the show. This is not an optimistic story and the crewmembers are not pals who never get in each other's face. There's tension in the air as the crew instinctively knows that their chances of surviving another year are slim at best.

In spite of the complicated storyline and the moving in and out of scenes of the various characters, Tasha Yar emerges as the focal point to which everyone returns. Even when the Enterprise-C meets up with the Enterprise-D, Tasha Yar is the one who takes a personal involvement in their fate, as well as in one of its crewmen, Lt. Richard Castillo. Their affair, if it can be called that, is brief and intense, coming as it does in the brief moments of peace they have in-between the even more intense moments of crisis. But even the character of Castillo is brushed with some sense of depth, so we don't feel as though Tasha has just fallen for a pretty face.

CHARACTER SUPPORT

Richard Castillo and Tasha Yar are both Starfleet officers encountering the most difficult challenge of their lives. When Tasha kisses Castillo as he is preparing to beam back to the Enterprise-C for the last time, the moment seems right and natural, not forced. And when Tasha reports for duty on the Enterprise-C, the pain in Castillo's face as he realizes that she has come to die at his side is very real, if unspoken. Much of the developing relationship between these two characters is communicated in their eyes and their facial expressions even more than with their words.

Even Whoopi Goldberg as Guinan gets to do a bit more than usual. While we ordinarily see her in Ten Forward listening to other people's problems and dispensing free advice along with her special alcohol-free drinks, she moves from passive to active status by confronting the situation she suspects. The scenes when she initially meets Tasha Yar are of particular interest as Guinan conveys subtle feelings of disquiet as she encounters someone she'd only known from computer records, and whom she knew to have died in the line of duty.

Because we know so little about Guinan, we accept the fact that she is at the eye of the storm, at the calm, unchanging center when time shifts. Since she is of an alien species we know little about, we believe that she would be essentially unchanged by what has happened. Even Data suggests that, "Perhaps her species has a perception that goes beyond linear time." Her people may well understand the nature of time better than anyone else in the Federation, and be able to resist a flux which alters everyone else's reality.

Jean Luc-Picard apparently understands this as well, which is why he accepts Guinan's observations even though on their face they should appear to be fantastic. Picard, war weary as he is portrayed here, takes the

chance, his last chance, and gambles that she may be right as he and the Enterprise face an otherwise inescapable fate.

What emerges is one of the best episodes of a science fiction series ever done for television as it balances a challenging storyline with good characterization to show how it can be pulled off when the pressure is really applied to everyone involved, particularly to the characters themselves.

CHAPTER 11

Star Trek postulates a future without racial barriers. In our own age barriers have fallen in major ways; here Levar Burton and Patrick Stewart celebrate at the wedding of Marina Sirtis on June 21, 1992.

Photo credit: Albert Ortega, ©1992 Ron Galella Ltd.

Ageism can also be a barrier—either against old or young.
Here Wil Wheaton attends the 1987 premiere of "Like Father—Like Son".

Photo credit: James Smeal, ©1987 Ron Galella Ltd.

By its nature, science fiction has often been a platform for taking a stand on various social issues by portraying 20th century events in a futuristic setting with a futuristic twist. STAR TREK has done its share of this and a certain fifth season NEXT GENERATION episode went where no science fiction TV show has ever gone before.

CHAPTER 11

"THE OUTCAST"— THE NATURE OF HUMAN RIGHTS

By James Van Hise

"The STAR TREK vision of the future presumes positive changes in behavior and attitudes. We've established that the planet will be free of discrimination and bias by that time so the question we'll address is what homosexuals will be like in the 24th Century."

— Gene Roddenberry

One of the precepts of STAR TREK which Gene Roddenberry believed that the series should always stick to was the sanctity of life. He felt that even when the Enterprise encountered some sort of monster, that the creature would clearly have its own reasons for committing anti-social acts. The Trek Classic episode "Devil In The Dark" is a prime example of that. "The Corbomite Maneuver" is another as that story introduced an alien monster and tricked us by having us react to the creature as though it were just an ugly alien—until the end when we discovered that it, too, had its reasons for acting the way it did and that nothing was as it really seemed. But the basic issue was that even an unusual entity was worthy of consideration and respect. Being strange or outside the norm was not automatically bad.

In STAR TREK: THE NEXT GENERATION, this was exemplified right from the start when the crew was shown to have an android crewman, Data, and a Klingon crewman, Worf. You can't get much more cosmopolitan than that while still maintaining a humanoid crew. By postulating that different is not automatically bad, STAR TREK was setting itself up for a 24th century conundrum. If this philosophy was true, why was the subject of gay crew members never addressed? The reason, of course, was that the series may take place in the 24th century, but the viewers, advertisers and ratings are all figured in 20th century terms, and portraying a gay character in even a neutral way, and not taking a position positive or negative, invites controversy. But this is not to say that it hadn't been considered.

As far back as 1976 I saw STAR TREK actors, who were appearing at conventions, and occasionally they were questioned by audience members as to why no gay crew members were ever shown on the TV series, as though the actors somehow had some sort of control over such creative decisions. The fact that STAR TREK was merely an artifact at that point also made the

question strictly moot.

NEW STAR TREK —NEW DILEMMAS

When STAR TREK returned in the form of movies in 1979, and then as THE NEXT GENERATION in 1987, the question was renewed in force. It was renewed in particular by David Gerrold, a co-creator of THE NEXT GENERATION (Geordi and Data were largely his ideas). Gerrold wrote an unproduced script in which a space plague with an AIDS parallel was encountered. The script also had a pair of gay crewmen presented in a casual manner. Gerrold left the series in 1987 to pursue the possible production of his own show, but then a subsequent falling-out he had with Roddenberry precluded Gerrold's script ever being produced.
However, the idea had been raised and Roddenberry had thought about it. He was still thinking about it in the months before his death. Roddenberry died when the fifth season of THE NEXT GENERATION was in production, but he had already gone in record as stating his clear intention to have gay crewmen portrayed on the Enterprise. That it was never overtly instituted has more to do with the timorous nature of the show's actual producers than on any sort of backing off on Roddenberry's part.

In the April 18, 1993 issue of the LOS ANGELES TIMES MAGAZINE, Ernest C. Over, who had been Roddenberry's personal assistant, responded to an item which had appeared in the TIMES implying that Roddenberry had broken his stated promise. Ernest first quoted Roddenberry's published promise which stated, "In the fifth season of STAR TREK, viewers will see more of shipboard life in some episodes, which will, among other things, include gay crew members in day-to-day circumstances." Over then added, "I know this because Gene dictated it to me. For the last 3 1/2 years of his life, I was Gene's personal assistant. Gene and I often spoke of how STAR TREK would portray lesbian and gay characters once an appropriate story line was found. Just prior to his death, at the beginning of the fifth season, Roddenberry told the ADVOCATE: 'The STAR TREK vision of the future presumes positive changes in behavior and attitudes. We've established that the planet will be free of discrimination and bias by that time so the question we'll address is what homosexuals will be like in the 24th Century.' Gene died before his plan could be carried out."

But it was attempted, albeit in an odd sideways fashion, and with mixed results. The fifth season episode in question is "The Outcast," written by Jeri Taylor, who was also the show's supervising producer. The episode was directed by Robert Scheerer. It guest stars Melinda Culea, Callan White and Megan Cole. Says Taylor, "I really wanted to write this episode. It came out of staff discussion. We had wanted to do a gay rights story and had not been able to figure out how to do it in

an interesting science fiction, STAR TREK-ian way. I came up with the idea of turning it on its ear and I really wanted to do it because, partly, it would be controversial and I welcome that. The idea of any drama is to touch people's feelings and engage them, whether you make them laugh, cry, angry. As long as you stir something in them, then you've been successful and I knew this would touch a lot of buttons in a lot of people.

"I am not a gay person," Taylor explains, "but as a woman I know what it feels like to be disenfranchised—not in that precise way—and I felt that I had a touchstone to some of the feelings that must be involved. On a personal level I wanted to write it. It's the episode of the whole two years I'm the most proud of and the most glad that I could be associated with. We've gotten every range of response, but largely positive."

THE NATURE OF GENDER

"The Outcast" opens on Stardate 45614.6. The Enterprise has been contacted by the J'Naii, an androgynous race. The J'Naii need assistance in locating a missing shuttle. Some of the J'Naii have beamed over and are on board helping in the search. In the process they discover an area of null space in the region which had never previous need detected.

Riker has been working with the aliens in the investigation, and his partner is a J'Naii named Soren. She's a specialist with pilot training so that she'll be able to fly the shuttlecraft they intend to use to penetrate the area of null space to see if the missing J'Naii shuttle is trapped inside. But first they must chart the pocket so they know exactly what they're getting into.

The J'Naii are a species without gender, but Riker likes the androgen he's working with. Not everyone on the Enterprise likes the J'Naii, though. Worf in particular is made uncomfortable by being around the androgynous people. Soren is coy but curious. She asks Riker what gender is like, something he finds difficult to explain. This scene is awkward as Soren asks Riker what a male is and he responds with a quip which couldn't possibly make sense to anyone who isn't from Earth.

Finally he explains that males tend to be bigger and have greater upper body strength. When he asks Soren what it is like to live on a planet where they have no gender, Soren's response isn't any more illuminating. Soren just basically says that it is all she has ever known. The scene doesn't accomplish very much up until the point that Soren asks Riker what kind of woman he is drawn to. Riker actually deals honestly with the question, stating what his interests are and discusses the intangibles of personal likes and dislikes.

FACING DANGER AS EQUALS

When Riker and Soren take the shuttle out to chart the pocket of null space, Soren inquires about human mating practices. Soren asks the

commander about his sexual organs, which startles him at first as he admits that it's not a normal subject for casual conversation. Riker explains that mating brings sexual closeness. Soren describes the mating practices of the J'Naii, and while he finds it a bit off-putting, Soren explains that there is a great deal of pleasure involved in the ritual.

Suddenly the shuttle encounters trouble and loses an engine. The turbulence throws Soren to the floor where she's knocked unconscious. Soren is beamed to Sickbay but the J'Naii only has a minor concussion. Initially when Soren is examined by Dr. Crusher the J'Naii appears nervous, but this soon passes. Soren asks Dr. Crusher what it's like to be female and she tries to explain but basically says that it is the way she has always been. Dr. Crusher states that long ago the female used to be considered inferior to the male, but that is no longer true. When Riker comes to see Soren in Sickbay, her unspoken response to him makes it evident to Dr. Crusher that Soren is attracted to Will Riker.

This leads into the next scene, a poker game in which the subject of male vs. female comes up. This happens when Deanna Troi declares certain cards wild and Worf labels it a woman's hand because wild cards make a weak hand stronger. When Dr. Crusher points out that this implies that Worf finds women weaker, the Klingon security chief casually agrees. This leads into Crusher's revelation that Soren seems to be attracted to Will Riker. Worf admits that the J'Naii make him uncomfortable because they are all the same, but he can't verbalize his feelings any more articulately than that.

Alone with Riker, Soren confesses affection for him. This is when we really start to understand the parallels being drawn by this story, and what is being set up. Soren explains that she was "born different" and is a throwback to the time when her people were born with gender and had a tendency to be male or female. But now the J'Naii consider gender to be offensive. The J'Naii feel that by evolving away from gender they have moved onto a higher form of life.

Soren explains that on her world such a thing as a strong inclination to one gender or the other is forbidden. Those found out to possess such feelings are ridiculed and given psycho treatments. Soren has lived with the secret of her having female gender emotions for a long time, living a life of pretense and lies. Clearly this is tackling the cultural life of this world head on as the "belief" that a race without gender is a higher form of life doesn't necessarily make it so. One also has to wonder how the J'Naii at large feel about dealing with a Federation ship which is filled with races who have different genders.

SOREN'S SECRET

Soren relates a painful childhood experience when one of her classmates was discovered to favor the male gender. He was ridiculed, tormented and even beaten up until the

authorities discovered it and the boy was taken away. When the child returned, the J'Naii stood before the assembled students in the school and explained how much better it felt after having been cured. Soren was terrified by this and knew that she had to keep the truth of her gender orientation a secret. "I have had to live a life of pretense and lies," she tells Riker.

By this time it is obvious what is going on and it is surprising in light of how studiously STAR TREK had avoided tackling this issue in any form. The parallels drawn bring to mind Earth in the early and mid-twentieth century as the actual gay rights movement which has been making a lot of news in 1993 didn't exist until 1969 when a police raid on a New York City bar called The Stonewall caused demonstrations and organized protest.

Before this (and certainly it is true to a large degree today) gays had to hide the truth about themselves and remain secretive. Homosexuality was labeled a psychiatric disorder until the 1970's, and the debate over gays in the military in 1993 has demonstrated that many people wish the issue had never come out of the closet. This was also demonstrated by some of the viewer reaction to this episode of THE NEXT GENERATION.

Riker and Soren take the shuttle out again and penetrate the area of null space. They find the J'Naii shuttle and rescue its two unconscious inhabitants and then are beamed back to the Enterprise when their own shuttle starts experiencing trouble.

Noor, the J'Naii leader, holds a

banquet in honor of the Enterprise for rescuing the shuttle crew. Riker and Soren go off alone in the woods and kiss. This is obviously a pretty reckless thing to do since Riker knows that what he and Soren are doing is forbidden on that world. Did he really think they wouldn't be discovered? While we're not told that they were seen, it is right after this that Soren is arrested and taken into custody.

Back on board the Enterprise, Riker goes to Troi and confesses his relationship with Soren. But Deanna had already noticed and isn't surprised. When Riker goes to Soren's temporary quarters on the ship he finds that Soren is gone and instead Krite is there in her place. Krite reveals that they know about Soren and Riker and Soren has been taken into custody.

JUDGMENT DAY

Riker beams down and bursts into the hearing where Soren is being tried for her social crime. To his credit, Riker stands up for Soren and takes the blame himself for what happened and states that he forced himself on Soren. But Soren decides to stop hiding and says that Riker is just trying to help. Soren confesses that she is female. This is the scene which everything else has been building up to as Soren stands up for herself and defends what she is. "I am tired of lies," she admits. "I have had these feelings, these longings, all of my life. It is not unnatural. I am not sick because I feel this way. I do not need to be helped. I do not need to be cured. What I need,

and what all of those who are like me need, is your understanding and your compassion."

Soren states that she has never done anything to hurt anyone and that her kind are scorned only because they are different. "All of the loving things that you do with each other, that is what we do. And for that we are called misfits and deviants. What right do you have to punish us? What right do you have to change us? What makes you think you can dictate how people love each other?" Soren demands. By this time any doubts the audience has had about what metaphor this episode is attempting to draw have all been resolved.

Unfortunately it is handled in a rather heavy handed fashion since Soren's speech is how the point is made and the concept addressed. Unlike David Gerrold's early plan to just have a couple gay crew members portrayed as being as normal and natural on the Enterprise as everyone else there is, here we get speeches about the rights of individuality.

The judge isn't impressed by the speech and in fact Noor has no doubt heard similar things before. The judge replies, "Your decision to admit your perversion makes it much more likely that we can help you."

While Soren is being led away, Riker steps up to the judge and objects, offering to take Soren back to the Enterprise never to return to trouble the J'Naii society. But Noor, the judge, explains that on this world everyone wants to be normal, and the J'Naii take their responsibilities to their people very seriously. For the Federation to interfere would violate the Prime Directive. Back on the Enterprise Riker meets with Picard to discuss the situation. Will Riker feels guilty about all this and blames himself, and well he should, for while Soren initiated the initial romance, Riker was the one who was reckless enough to kiss Soren on the surface of her own world. Picard counsels Riker against doing anything rash but he won't stand in Will's way.

THE DEFIANT ONE

Riker plans an escape attempt and Worf offers to help. The Klingon has come to terms with his discomfort. While he had initially disliked the J'Naii he respects the idea of individuality. Plus he is loyal to Riker and states, "A warrior does not let a friend face danger alone."

They beam down but when they rescue Soren, it's too late. She's already been brainwashed and claims to be happy. When Riker tells Soren that maybe Dr. Crusher can reverse the treatment, Soren is surprised at the suggestion and rejects it. Why would she want to go back to the way she was? Soren's personality has largely altered and with it any feelings she had for Riker have been neutralized. Regretfully, Riker agrees to Soren's wishes and he returns to the Enterprise without her.

Riker resumes his post on the bridge where Captain Picard states that they are scheduled to proceed to the Phelah system unless his first

officer needs more time. Riker replies that his business with the J'Naii has been concluded.

INSIDE THE OUTCAST

The approach to the subject taken in the episode is pretty timorous. By having the story be an analogy, and almost a parable, the producers tried to have it both ways. It's a gay themed story, but it isn't. It plays on both levels. Certainly a lot of younger fans wouldn't have picked up on what was really going on here, but some would have. Gay teens would have and for that reason the big speech scene is probably important in this regard because it's a defense made by a person for the way they were born, and it is an articulate defense.

It puts into words the feelings that a gay teen would be trying to come to grips with. Often when a gay themed storyline is censored it is done in the name of "family values." (This happened with the recent storyline in the newspaper strip "For Better Or For Worse" in which a fifteen year old boy confesses that he is gay and the story portrays the impact that this revelation has on the people around him. Those few newspapers who declined to present it argued that they are a "family" newspaper in spite of the fact that this is a vital issue for families to come to grips with, not to hide from). Some fans were annoyed at the way the storyline played out in "The Outcast" since Riker never once mentions how similar this is to what life used to be like on Earth for gay people in the 20th century. While intellectually it would make sense for him to come to that conclusion, dramatically that would come across like the viewer was being beaten over the head with the theme. So while on one hand it would seem obvious for Riker to mention it, on the other hand it would have made everything too obvious if he had. Doing a story line like this is a tightrope walk anyway and it is better to err on the side of restraint rather than come across as being shrill. Otherwise you're just preaching to the converted.

Another criticism I heard was that it seemed convenient that the androgynous race of the J'Naii were all played by actresses rather than actors. Imagine how much more unnerving the show would have been had the J'Naii been portrayed by androgynous looking males with slight builds, sort of the way the male Eloi were portrayed in the 1960 motion picture THE TIME MACHINE. But this, too, would have made the story line a bit too tough to take for many fans, particularly since Riker has been shown to be quite a womanizer. Some fans were even offended by the scenes in "The Game" where Riker, early in the episode, looks at the woman who is keeping him company on leave as though she is nothing more than pretty meat.

POSITIVE FEEDBACK

While there was some negative fan reaction to the storyline (both out of homophobia and because some fans resent when anything resembling

reality intrudes on their fantasy entertainments), it garnered some very positive reactions as well.

In the August 1992 issue of STARLOG, two letters addressed this episode in a positive fashion. Charles L. Cranford IV of Greensboro, North Carolina wrote in part that while the story line didn't really address the concept of having a gay crew member head on, he understood that it was at least a beginning as it was a subject STAR TREK had never dealt with in its more than 25 years of existence. "But I do admire TNG's courage in taking this first step in presenting this sensitive subject indirectly," Crandord added. "I do hold out hope, however, that in the coming months of the new season, TNG will slowly introduce a secondary gay or lesbian character. I believe that this would not only serve my cause, to bring gay men and lesbians the respect and understanding we deserve, but will also serve TNG's viewers by showing that in the 24th century, all social, political, religious, ethnic, racial, sexual and sexual orientation bias and prejudice have been eliminated."

While the other letter in that issue of STARLOG on "The Outcast" was essentially positive, Richard Van Frank of Montclair, New Jersey felt that it was undermined by having Riker falling into the arms of someone yet again, something which happens so often that his relationships are difficult to take seriously. Frank said that "The Outcast" was: "exceptionally well-conceived as a story, in principle. Jeri Taylor addressed the timely, sensitive and difficult issue of sexual preference with taste and intelligence. Dealing with a controversial theme fits well into the general fabric of TNG, and can bring out a significant point and message. Jonathan Frakes was at his best. What a pity Taylor couldn't refrain from the TNG writers' increasing inability to keep Riker's fly closed."

In the July/August bulletin of STAR TREK—The Official Fan Club, there are also two letters dealing with "The Outcast." Jan Thomas of Lebanon, Ohio addresses a number of points when he states: "I'm sure the gay community wouldn't think they did justice to their plight, but as an observer from the other side, it made me see the idea of sexuality as a very personal and private thing. Not something that can be judged right or wrong in another's point of view. If only a few people viewed this episode and were moved to consider the freedom of another to choose partners as their personal rights and not an infringement on everyone, then the show accomplished something important. Few television shows are afforded this opportunity."

DEAR STAR TREK —STAY IN THE CLOSET

Taking the opposite point of view is Steven D. De Lacy from Costa Mesa, California. In a long letter, among his other points, De Lacy complains, "Well, it's my turn to cry

foul to the writers and producers of STAR TREK who would allow an episode with this message so slanted to one extreme that it reduced the show to a mere soapbox for one group's political agenda to be voiced. We all know that this story was meant as an analogy to our own society today."

De Lacy continues on about this for several more paragraphs (while never once directly addressing the issue by using the word "gay" or "homosexual") and then concludes: "There are so many other television shows that already lean whichever way the politically correct wind happens to blow; it would seem from the episode "The Outcast" that the only differences between these shows and STAR TREK are pretty sets and special effects."

What De Lacy doesn't address is that STAR TREK studiously avoided confronting this issue in any form for more than 25 years, and when they did choose to address it, the writers tackled it from a human rights stand point, demonstrating what happens when morality collides with human rights. This reduces it to a moral versus an ethical consideration, for while morality dictates a "proper" way to do something, ethics deals with what is actually "right" and honorable. The two words are not as interchangeable as some might think.

In the September/October 1992 issue of the bulletin, a fan wrote in to respond De Lacey. Donna Roazen of Westfield, Massachusetts addressed the point made, stating, "What I saw was the advocacy of tolerance, of recognizing that in sexual matters as well as in all others, we are a diverse society." She concludes by stating, "My ounce of intelligence tells me that rather than promoting homosexuality, The Outcast sought to examine the mentality demonstrated by Mr. DeLacey and those who share his views. It is my hope that STAR TREK will continue to show us a world in which some day, we will truly respect the other's right to be an individual. If anyone cares, I am heterosexual. But not, thank God, a homophobe."

THE RODDENBERRY PHILOSOPHY

While it took STAR TREK a long time to address this particular issue, it's not because Roddenberry hadn't been thinking about it. A card carrying member of the American Civil Liberties Union, Roddenberry was an unapologetic liberal, and this was a subject he'd thought about for a very long time before coming forward and stating that he finally intended to have STAR TREK deal with it. His first public statement on the subject actually occurred in the mid-seventies in the book SHATNER: WHERE NO MAN by William Shatner, Sondra Marshak and Myrna Culbreath. Roddenberry is quoted in a discussion about whether he ever considered the possibility of Kirk and Spock being lovers.

Said Roddenberry, "There's

certainly some of that with—certainly with love overtones. Deep love. The only difference being, the Greek ideal—we never suggested in the series—physical love between the two. But it's the—we certainly had the feeling the affection was sufficient for that, if that were the particular style in the 23rd century." (He looks thoughtful). "That's very interesting. I never thought of that before."

Roddenberry didn't dismiss the idea and in 1991 he gave the interview to THE ADVOCATE which was quoted earlier in this chapter. STAR TREK has always been a platform for ideas which explore the human equation, and the humane aspects of it, whether it involves humans or aliens. This is what STAR TREK has always represented, and the episode "The Outcast" for STAR TREK: THE NEXT GENERATION carries on that tradition admirably.

CHAPTER 12

Jonathan Frakes on stage at a Star Trek convention.

Photo credit: Albert Ortega, ©1992 Ron Galella Ltd.

Jonathan Frakes at the Hotel Nikko Grand Open Education First held Feb. 10, 1992.

Encountering a double has been done before on STAR TREK, both in the original series and on THE NEXT GENERATION. But in the sixth season episode "Second Chances" a fresh approach was taken in which the double was neither evil, nor did he die at the end!

CHAPTER 12

DUELING RIKERS

By T.S. Braxton

It could have been a cliché— after all, how many times did a duplicate Kirk lead to trouble back on the first spacefaring Enterprise? But when Commander Riker encountered his own double in the sixth season NEXT GENERATION episode entitled "Second Chances," it's not just another evil twin story, or yet another guess-the-impostor conundrum— it's a very intriguing drama. Riker quite literally meets himself. . . but a self whose life has followed a considerably different course than his own has for the past eight years.

While there is some initial friction between the two Rikers, they are not enemies. The second Riker is not out to take over the Enterprise or to do in his counterpart, he just wants to get on with his own life. So does the Riker that we've known since "Encounter At Farpoint." And this is where the drama in "Second Chances" comes into play. No clichés, no reruns of previous scenarios, and a tendency to run counter to the devices we usually expect from a STAR TREK episode are what set "Second Chances" above the average NEXT GENERATION story. In the otherwise general decline of the sixth season of the series which only started picking up in the second half of the season, this episode stands out as one of the best in recent years.

As the second-in-command of Picard's Enterprise, Will Riker was of course a key character in Roddenberry's re-visioning of the structure of command in the STAR TREK universe. Whereas Kirk would generally beam down to any hostile planet himself despite the risk, Starfleet protocol (and centuries of historical precedent) dictates that the commanding officer of a vessel should never place himself at risk. But more than this, Commander Riker has evolved into an important character in THE NEXT GENERATION, a character with quite a history— a history which is crucial to an understanding of the events in "Second Chances."

Like all the other regular crew members in TNG except Lieutenant Worf, Riker was first seen in "Encounter At Farpoint," in which he was the officer that the Enterprise went to Farpoint to pick up. Upon beaming up to the Enterprise, however, Riker was surprised to find that the ship's Counselor was Deanna Troi, with whom he had once been involved several years earlier. They set their romantic past aside and resumed a platonic friendship, while sometimes still thinking of what once had been.

PATHS NOT TAKEN

Riker's feelings are not entirely buried. He was certainly a bit perturbed when, in the episode "Haven," he discovered that Deanna was going to go through with an arranged wedding. He was secretly pleased when the match, set up by Lwaxana Troi, fell through. Riker's desire for female companionship often leads to entanglements of a less than platonic nature, but in fact he probably wishes that his active pursuit of his Starfleet career did not put a damper on his immediate chances of developing any stable, long-term relationship. In the episode "11001001," he was rather disappointed to discover that the fascinating woman Minuet was merely a holodeck program, and one which he

was unable to recreate to his satisfaction.

Riker's old feelings for Deanna were again given a bit of a jolt when she became pregnant by a space creature seeking incarnation in "The Child." This gives further evidence that Riker is, if nothing else, flexible in his thinking, at least as long as something doesn't hit too close to home.

Riker's ambitious nature certainly came into full play in "A Matter of Honor," when he jumped at the chance to be the first Starfleet Commander to serve as an exchange officer on board a Klingon vessel. This situation called for Riker's reflexes and thinking to be at their peak form, as he was not only obliged to acquire a taste for Klingon food, but also to repel the advances of Klingon women, one variety of female that doesn't seem to appeal to the usually libidinous first officer.

But Riker's ambition is tempered by his loyalty to Captain Picard, and the belief that he can learn a lot on board the Enterprise. In "The Icarus Factor," his estranged father Kyle Riker came on board to tell the younger that he had been offered the captaincy of the Ares. Kyle pressured Will to take this job; he was disappointed that his son had already passed up an opportunity to command his own vessel. This revived an old conflict between the two, who hadn't spoken in fifteen years. The episode examines their troubled relationship. Will agonized over the captaincy he'd been offered, but ultimately he passed it up, since he would have been taking it more to impress his father than because he was really ready for it.

SKILLS AND CHOICES

Riker is also a consummate poker player. In "The Price," his poker playing skills led Picard to make him the Federation's replacement negotiator in a crucial trade treaty conference. But the real danger at the table was a secret Betazoid who was misusing his powers to gain an edge as well as to romance Deanna Troi. When this individual tried to manipulate Riker's feelings for Deanna, he misjudged them and failed.

In "The Vengeance Factor," Riker found a troublesome romance with an Acamar servant, Yuta, but was forced to kill her in a dramatic confrontation when she as revealed as an assassin who could not be stopped by any other means.

Riker's sense of humor came into play when he asked Captain Picard to bring him back a certain souvenir from Rysa in "Captain's Holiday." This was actually a practical joke: the item was really a Rysan signal of sexual availability. As might be expected, the meticulous Picard bought Riker's "gift" the moment he arrived on Rysa, then settled down for a peaceful vacation reading James Joyce's ULYSSES. It took awhile for Picard to figure out why his reading was being interrupted by an endless stream of beautiful women. Riker's prank was certainly a success, but even Riker would never have guessed the nature of the adventure that it would lead Picard into.

In "The Best of Both Worlds," Riker took command of the Enterprise when Picard was kidnapped and transformed into the Borg, Locutus. Here Riker demonstrated his leadership in a battle situation, actually giving the order to fire on Locutus' ship, and eventually outwitting the memories of his own mentor in the final battle with the Borg.

"Future Imperfect" found Riker awakening after sixteen years to find himself the captain of the Enterprise, with a son. He had somehow forgotten the sixteen years in question. His last memory was of a visit to a planet, where he was infected by a virus that lay dormant for years until wiping out all memories accrued since its inception. In the Philip K. Dick tradition, apparent reality takes several sharp turns before the truth is revealed. But it was his captors' error in using Minuet as his wife that led him to break free of the apparent Romulan trap that he had fallen into.

In one of the most trying adventures of his career, Riker was wounded in the course of a secret cultural observation in the episode "First Contact." Taken to a Malkorian hospital, his "alien" nature was soon revealed, and the mission was seriously compromised. Aid came in the form of a Malkorian (Bebe

Neuwirth) who helps him escape in return for some intergalactic passion. If nothing else, Riker is graceful under pressure.

In "The Host," Riker once again put his life on the line by allowing an alien symbiont to be temporarily placed in his body. There seems to be no risk that this man is unwilling to take if the stakes are high enough. But throughout this and his various other adventures, he has never encountered anything like the events of "Second Chances."

A MAN OF TWO MINDS

Appearing late in the sixth season, this unusual twist on an otherwise familiar idea was based on a story by Michael A. Medlock with the final teleplay written by series veteran Rene Echevarria. The episode marks the directorial debut of LeVar Burton.

The story begins deceptively enough as Enterprise approaches Nervala-Four, a planet surrounded by a distortion field which makes transporting to and from the service of that world difficult. Only when the planet's orbit takes it close enough to its sun does it become possible to find low enough levels of distortion to transport through. This happens about every eight years. Eight years earlier, an Away Team from the Potemkin had rescued the inhabitants of a science station on the planet. The leader of that team, Lieutenant Will Riker, had been the last to beam up, and had almost failed to make it back. Commended for his efforts, Riker was

quickly promoted, thus hastening his progress to his present post on the Enterprise.

As the Enterprise reaches orbit, Riker is in Ten Forward, leading a jazz band while an appreciative audience, including Beverly Crusher and Deanna Troi, listens. When Riker asks for requests, Deanna calls out the title "Night Bird." Riker pretends not to hear her, and asks for requests again. She asks for "Night Bird" again, but no one else has any other requests, and so he is stuck with performing that song. As the band begins, Deanna explains that Riker has been working on the song for a decade, but has never been able to get through the trombone solo without making a mistake. Just as Riker is about to join in with the other musicians, he is called to the bridge— much to his relief.

On the bridge, Data and Riker discuss the situation. Their mission is to retrieve the scientific information left behind in the computer database on Nervala-Four eight years earlier. Improvements in Transporters in the past few years make the job a bit easier, but even so there will only be three Transporter "windows" over the next several days. If the database is not retrieved in this time, it will have to wait another eight years.

The first window, which will last twenty-six minutes, arrives, and Riker beams down to the science station with Data and Worf. It seems that someone has been maintaining the station, which was a shambles when Riker last saw it. Worf speculates that a spaceship might have crashed there. Data detects an approaching humanoid life form with his tricorder. Drawing their phasers as a precaution, they watch as the figure steps from the shadows. It is Will Riker, dressed in a tattered yellow lieutenant's uniform!

The two Rikers stare at each other, dumbfounded.

NO QUESTION— THEY'RE BOTH WILL RIKER!

They begin to quiz each other. Both believe that they are the Will Riker, and rejects the other one's claim. Sensing an impasse in this conversation, Data steps in and asks Lieutenant Riker how he got there. Lieutenant Riker recounts the story of how he led the Away Team from the Potemkin eight years earlier. His version differs in one important detail: the distortion field kept him from being able to beam up, and he has long assumed that he was left for dead.

Lieutenant Riker agrees to a medical examination, and beams up to sickbay with Worf. Dr. Crusher finds him in good health, although she detects that one of his arms had been broken and healed; he admits that he had to set it himself. Picard arrives to meet the new arrival and questions Crusher about him. Could he be a clone? Crusher doubts it, as there is no genetic drift detected in her exam. Not only is Lieutenant Riker genetically identical to

Commander Riker, his brain patterns are also the same, with slight differences easily accounted for by eight years of different experiences. Lieutenant Riker is the same person as the Commander, although he exists separately— but how?

Geordi LaForge checks out the Transporter logs from the Potemkin and believes he has found the answer to that question. The officers assemble in Picard's conference room as Geordi explains. When the Potemkin was beaming Riker back up, its Transporter chief had trouble getting a lock on Riker's signal, so he boosted the transport beam with a second containment field, apparently intending to reintegrate the fields at the beam-in point. Riker beamed up in the first beam, and the second one was shut down. But it too had picked up Riker, and somehow the second beam reflected off the distortion field surrounding the planet, beaming Riker back down to the science station at the same time that he was also beaming back up to the Potemkin! There's no getting around it— both Rikers are real. This news gives Deanna Troi food for thought.

Another Away Team is planned to go after the database. Picard suggests that they take Lieutenant Riker along, since he did a lot of reconfiguration on the station computer, removing components and using them to keep the station's radiation shields operational. Deanna volunteers to go to Lieutenant Riker's quarters and ask him if he's willing to join the mission.

GONE BUT NOT FORGOTTEN

When Deanna enters his quarters, she hardly has time to ask him anything, as he takes her in his arms and kisses her passionately.

Deanna draws back and tries to explain how her feelings for Commander Riker have changed. Lieutenant Riker remembers their last meeting as lovers, at the Generan falls on Beta-Zed. There they promised to meet on Rysa in six weeks. The meeting never took place. For Lieutenant Riker, this has one meaning. But Deanna tells him that Commander Riker never made it, either, as his career on the Potemkin moved so fast after the Nervala-Four rescue that he never had a chance to reunite with Deanna until they both joined the crew of the Enterprise.

Lieutenant Riker points out that, while his counterpart may have given up his passion for Deanna, he has not. In fact, it was the thought of seeing her again that kept him going throughout all his years as a castaway.

Deanna changes the subject and asks Lieutenant Riker if he will join the Away Team. He says that he will. But as she goes to leave, he reminds her that his feeling have not changed since they last met on Beta-Zed.

MY BROTHER, MYSELF

Lieutenant Riker is late for the beam down, and Commander Riker is angry. Apparently Lr. Riker hasn't adjusted to living on someone else's schedule again. Down on the planet, the Lieutenant explains that he had rerouted most of the computer lines. They cannot retrieve anything from the consoles; Lieutenant Riker had shunted the database to the central computer core beneath the station.

He crawls under a console to see if he can access the core database. As he works, Commander Riker wonders if they should tell their father that he now has two sons. Lieutenant Riker doesn't really think its necessary— he has no desire to see his father again. But he's curious about how Commander Riker got in touch with Kyle Riker. Commander Riker explains about the time he was offered the Ares. Lieutenant Riker cannot believe that Commander Riker turned down that captaincy. Obviously, the two Rikers can find little to agree upon.

Lieutenant Riker discovers that the primary computer coupling is fused. There can be no link-up with the core, and it seems that the servo-link with the subterranean computer core has probably been damaged by the frequent seismic activity on Nervala-Four. There's no time to go down and fix it, however, as the Transporter window is about to end. Lieutenant Riker wants to stay and work on it; he'll be done by the time of the third window. Commander Riker vetoes this idea; the caverns are too unstable. Lieutenant Riker tries to stay anyway, but Commander Riker pulls rank on him, and they all beam up to the Enterprise.

Deanna receives a note from Lieutenant Riker, which gives her a clue that leads her to a Transporter room. There she finds a flower and another note. A series of notes and clues leads her to various locations ending with Ten Forward, where she meets Lieutenant Riker.

He gives her a gift: a piece of metal on which he has etched, with a phaser beam, a depiction of the Genaran Falls. (After all, he had a lot of time on his hands on Nervala-Four). They talk about "their" past and more recent events, and something in him reawakens Deanna's interest. She confesses how disappointed she was when Commander Riker never made their rendezvous on Rysa.

RIVALS FOR THE FUTURE?

Meanwhile, Picard tells Commander Riker that he's decided to go along with Lieutenant Riker's plan, despite the risk. Commander Riker agrees, but he is angry that Lieutenant Riker went over his head, and confronts the Lieutenant in engineering. The friction between them is strong, as if they cannot stand each other.

Later, Beverly Crusher and Deanna are in the gym, practicing the Klingon exercises taught to them by Worf. Crusher is quizzing Deanna on Lieutenant Riker's attentions to her.

Lieutenant Riker appears, and Crusher leaves the two alone. Lieutenant Riker notes the similarity between the Klingon exercises and Tai Chi Ch'uan. They begin to compare techniques. Deanna throws Lieutenant Riker to the floor and kisses him passionately.

Some time afterwards, Deanna talks to Commander Riker, who is concerned that Lieutenant Riker might make the same decision that he made, putting career before romance. His main concern is that Deanna will be hurt again.

That evening's poker game between Worf, Data and Commander Riker is interrupted by the arrival of Lieutenant Riker, who wants to talk to his alter-ego. Commander Riker invites him to join the poker game. It becomes a game of one-upsmanship between the two Rikers, with the Lieutenant raising the stakes long after Worf and Data have folded. But this grudge match ends when Commander Riker faces off Lieutenant Riker's bluff to the bitter end: ""I've practiced in the mirror too long to be fooled by that face."

A SURPRISE ENDING

Lieutenant Riker receives word that, with Picard's help, he has been assigned to a post on the Gandhi, and will transfer in one week. He will be allowed to take family on board after six months— will Deanna marry him? Deanna can't commit to that, as her work on the Enterprise is important to her. She understands that

Lieutenant Riker cannot stay on the same ship as Commander Riker, but she can't go with him, either. But when Lieutenant Riker asks her if their relationship is over, she tells him that it is not.

The Away Team beams down, and both Rikers go down to the computer core to repair it. Lieutenant Riker observes that there has been considerably more seismic damage since his last visit.

Meanwhile, Worf and Data discuss the unusual situation. Data wonders how Worf would react to meeting his double. Worf says that it would probably be difficult— he admits that he is hard to get along with. But Data observes that both Commander Riker and Lieutenant Riker are easy to get along with, yet they do not care for each other at all. Worf surmises that they probably are seeing something in each other that they don't like in themselves, and that this is what they are reacting to.

Lieutenant Riker and Commander Riker reach a catwalk that leads to the computer core. But as they are crossing it, it collapses, and Lieutenant Riker falls, only to be grabbed by Commander Riker. Both are in danger of tumbling into a vast chasm beneath them, and Commander Riker cannot pull Lieutenant Riker up unless Lieutenant Riker climbs. Lieutenant Riker tells Commander Riker to let him fall, but Commander Riker refuses, and they manage to get back to safety and repair the link to the computer core. Data and Worf

retrieve the information, and the Away Team is beamed back up with no mishaps.

Deanna and Lieutenant Riker say their farewells. It will be a long time, but matters are not yet closed between them. Lieutenant Riker has waited for her eight years— he can wait a little longer. Commander Riker gives Lieutenant Riker a trombone as a gesture of conciliation, and the Lieutenant— who will be using his middle name of Thomas from now on— leaves Deanna with Commander Riker, asking his alter-ego to take good care of her.

AND THEN, AND THEN. . .

Who would have thought that the episode would end like that? Never in the history of TV episodes dealing with doubles have the two become friends. Either they die, or seemingly die (as in "Datalore"), are evil twins who deserve to die ("Datalore" again, as well as "Mirror, Mirror") or the two halves of a whole ("The Enemy Within") are reunited.

"Second Chances" owes something to "The Enemy Within" for its inspiration since that first season episode of Classic Trek involves a duplicate Kirk being created from a Transporter malfunction. Although the two Kirks were reunited again, since neither half could function adequately without the other, it did open up the never explored possibility of what would happen had the two individuals truly been identical? Would disposing of one be murder? Although Trek Classic didn't deal with the concept of a perfect, human duplicate who wasn't a clone, THE NEXT GENERATION tackled it head on and never even considered disposing of one of them. After all, how would you decide which was the real Will Riker? Both clearly are real and one of them has survived for eight years, proving that the duplication was flawless.

The only shortcoming of the story is that both Will Rikers accept the existence of their double without a great deal of turmoil. Following the initial shock of their meeting face to face, they accept the cards fate has dealt them with quite a lot of equanimity. Although the two seem to get on each other's nerves, there is never any sort of blow up where one accuses the other of being his duplicate or demands to know which of them existed first..

The one point of real contention that might have existed between them is Deanna Troi. But Commander Will Riker's platonic interest in her only goes to point out the very real emotional differences between the two men. Lt. Riker is what Commander Riker might have been had he made different choices in life, and one of those choices was Deanna Troi. The fact that Deanna actually responds to Lt. Riker is far more interesting than had she remained distant and aloof. This whole episode captures the essence of what makes STAR TREK exciting, as it portrays a plausible future in which almost anything is possible,

particularly on a human level. One can only wonder what the future holds for Lt. Thomas Riker?

ORDER FORM

_____ Trek Crew Book $9.95
_____ Best Of Enterprise Incidents $9.95
_____ Trek Fans Handbook $9.95
_____ Trek: The Next Generation $14.95
_____ The Man Who Created Star Trek: $12.95
_____ 25th Anniversary Trek Tribute $14.95
_____ History Of Trek $14.95
_____ The Man Between The Ears $14.95
_____ Trek: The Making Of The Movies $14.95
_____ Trek: The Lost Years $12.95
_____ Trek: The Unauthorized Next Generation $14.95
_____ New Trek Encyclopedia $19.95
_____ Making A Quantum Leap $14.95
_____ The Unofficial Tale Of Beauty And The Beast $14.95
_____ Complete Lost In Space $19.95
_____ ..doctor Who Encyclopedia: Baker $19.95
_____ Lost In Space Tribute Book $14.95
_____ Lost In Space With Irwin Allen $14.95
_____ Doctor Who: Baker Years $19.95
_____ Doctor Who: Pertwee Years $19.95
_____ Batmania Ii $14.95
_____ The Green Hornet $14.95 _____ Special Edition $16.95

_____ Number Six: The Prisoner Book $14.95
_____ Gerry Anderson: Supermarionation $17.95
_____ Addams Family Revealed $14.95
_____ Bloodsucker: Vampires At The Movies $14.95
_____ Dark Shadows Tribute $14.95
_____ Monsterland Fear Book $14.95
_____ The Films Of Elvis $14.95
_____ The Woody Allen Encyclopedia $14.95
_____ Paul Mccartney: 20 Years On His Own $9.95
_____ Yesterday: My Life With The Beatles $14.95
_____ Fab Films Of The Beatles $14.95
_____ 40 Years At Night: The Tonight Show $14.95
_____ Exposing Northern Exposure $14.95
_____ The La Lawbook $14.95
_____ Cheers: Where Everybody Knows Your Name $14.95
_____ SNL! The World Of Saturday Night Live $14.95
_____ The Rockford Phile $14.95
_____ Encyclopedia Of Cartoon Superstars $14.95
_____ How To Create Animation $14.95
_____ How To Draw Art For Comic Books $14.95
_____ King And Barker:an Illustrated Guide $14.95
_____ King And Barker: An Illustrated Guide II $14.95

100% Satisfaction Guaranteed.

We value your support. You will receive a full refund as long as the copy of the book you are not happy with is received back by us in reasonable condition. No questions asked, except we would like to know how we failed you. Refunds and credits are given as soon as we receive back the item you do not want.

NAME:_____

STREET:_____

CITY:_____

STATE:_____

ZIP:_____

TOTAL:_____ SHIPPING_____
                              T: TRIB

SEND TO: Couch Potato, Inc. 5715 N. Balsam Rd., Las Vegas, NV 89130